Direct Selling Channels

Direct Selling Channels

Bert Rosenbloom
Editor

The Haworth Press, Inc.
New York • London • Norwood (Australia)

Direct Selling Channels has also been published as *Journal of Marketing Channels*, Volume 2, Number 2 1992.

The Haworth Press, Inc., 10 Alice Street, Binghamton, NY 13904-1580 USA

Library of Congress Cataloging-in-Publication Data

Direct selling channels / Bert Rosenbloom, editor.
     p. cm.
   "Has also been published as Journal of marketing channels Volume 2, Number 2 1992"-T.p. verso.
    Includes bibliographical references.
    ISBN 1-56024-445-3 (H : acid free paper).–ISBN 1-56024-446-1 (pbk. : acid free paper)
    1. Direct selling. 2. Consumers–Attitudes. I. Rosenbloom, Bert.
HF5438.25.D556 1992
658.8'4–dc20
                                                92-40395
                                                    CIP

Direct Selling Channels

CONTENTS

ABOUT THE EDITOR

Bert Rosenbloom, PhD, holds the G. Behrens Ulrich Professorship in Marketing at Drexel University. One of the world's leading experts on the management of marketing channels and distribution systems, Dr. Rosenbloom has also been an active consultant for a broad range of industries in manufacturing, wholesaling, retailing, communications, services, and real estate in the United States and abroad.

One of Dr. Rosenbloom's five books, *Marketing Channels: A Management View* (Holt, Rinehart and Winston), now going into its fourth edition, is the standard textbook in the field. Another of his books, *Retail Marketing* (Random House), a pioneering text on the application of modern marketing methods to retail channels, has had a major impact on distribution thought in the United States and in other countries around the world. His latest book, *Marketing Functions and the Wholesaler Distributor* (Distribution Research and Education Foundation) has been acclaimed in the wholesaling sector for providing the industry with new concepts and analytical methods for increasing productivity in wholesale marketing channels.

Dr. Rosenbloom's research has been widely published in the major scholarly journals of marketing such as the *Journal of Marketing, Journal of Retailing, Academy of Marketing Science Journal, Industrial Marketing Management, Journal of Consumer Marketing, Business Horizons, Journal of Personal Selling and Sales Management, Management Review, Long Range Planning,* and *European Journal of Marketing.* His research is also frequently presented at professional conferences of the American Marketing Association, European Marketing Association, Academy of Marketing Science, Decision Sciences Institute, World Marketing Congress, Retail Research Society, National Retail Merchants Association, Distribution Research and Education Foundation, Direct Selling Education Foundation, and many others in the United States and other countries around the world.

Dr. Rosenbloom serves on the editorial boards of the *Journal of Consumer Marketing, Journal of the Academy of Marketing Science, Journal of International Consumer Marketing,* and on the ad hoc review boards of the *Journal of Marketing Research, Journal of Marketing,* and the *Journal of Retailing.* He also served for nine years as Academic Consulting Editor for the Random House series of books on marketing. The recipient of the Erskine Fellowship in 1986, Dr. Rosenbloom was Vice President of the Philadelphia Chapter of the American Marketing Association and a member of the Board of Governors of the Academy of Marketing Science.

Dr. Rosenbloom is listed in *American Men and Women of Science, Who's Who in the East, Who's Who in the World, Contemporary Authors* and the *International Dictionary of Biography.*

Introduction

Direct selling, the distribution of consumer products and services through personal, face-to-face (salesperson-to-customer) sales away from fixed business locations has been an important marketing channel throughout the twentieth century, not only in the United States but in many other countries around the world. By the start of the present decade in the U.S. alone, direct selling channels accounted for $12 billion in sales volume produced by almost 5 million independent direct salespeople.

As we move toward the twenty-first century, prospects for continued viability and growth of direct selling channels are quite good, but some major challenges also face this particular marketing channel.

In an effort to bring together the latest, most-in-depth thought, analysis and research on the prospects and challenges for direct selling channels, the Direct Selling Education Foundation supported the development of this book. The articles appearing here represent the work of leading marketing scholars who have intensively studied and researched direct selling channels in recent years. The collection of articles presented thus represents state of the art thought and research on direct selling channels.

Enis leads off the collection with "Direct Selling Channels: An Appraisal of Key Strategic Issues." This article provides a concise, yet very insightful overview of the salient issues facing direct selling as distilled from a broad cross-section of leading direct selling industry executives as well as the published literature.

In "Consumer Responses to Direct Selling: Love, Hate . . . Buy?" Barnowe and McNabb provide research findings on what is perhaps the *most* fundamental factor affecting the future of direct selling–consumers' experiences with and attitudes toward direct selling methods.

Wotruba and Tyagi present a research study which also deals with one of the most basic issues in direct selling–why people decide to become direct salespeople in "Motivation to Become a Direct Salesperson and Its Relationship with Work Outcomes."

The fourth article, "The Role of Personal Selling in Direct Sales Organizations," by Ingram makes a strong case for bringing innovative concepts such as trust-based relationship selling into the mainstream of direct selling organizations.

Teer et al. present some fascinating research findings in "Sex-Role Self-Concept and Direct Sales Success in Minority Saleswomen," a study of the relationship between sex-role self-concept and sales performance in direct selling.

Direct selling in an international context is the focus of Schwartz's article, "Direct Selling: A Multinational Strategy." The author presents a novel and well-conceived method for identifying international markets for new products sold through direct selling channels.

In this final article, "Current Status and Future Directions for Research on Direct Selling Channels," Albaum presents a comprehensive review of the research-based literature on direct selling that has appeared during the decade. His critical appraisal of this work, augmented by a survey of direct selling executives, goes a long way in assessing the state of the art and providing direction for future research in direct selling channels.

As the editor of the *Journal of Marketing Channels*, I am very proud of this volume on *Direct Selling Channels*. I want to commend and thank all of the authors for the outstanding job they did in presenting a group of articles that makes a substantial contribution to the direct selling and marketing channel literature.

I would also like to take this opportunity to thank Marlene Futterman, Executive Director of the Direct Selling Education Foundation, as well as the Board of Directors of DSEF for their encouragement and support of this undertaking. I am confident that this collection of articles will enrich our understanding of direct selling channels and become a classic reference source for academics and practitioners interested in advancing knowledge and practice in direct selling.

Bert Rosenbloom

Direct Selling Channels:
An Appraisal
of Key Strategic Issues

Ben M. Enis

SUMMARY. Direct selling channels are changing. Throughout the world, customers, sales representatives, direct selling companies, and the societies in which they exist are changing rapidly. This paper examines changes in each of the above-mentioned major "players" in direct selling channels, and offers recommendations for strategies for managing these changes.

INTRODUCTION

To say that the world is changing is to voice a truism. For the Direct Selling industry, these changes can best be discussed in terms of four "players": customers, sales representatives, companies, and society in general. The challenge to senior executives and managers of firms in the direct selling industry is to (1) recognize significant change, (2) assess the impact of such change upon his/her company and industry, and (3) formulate strategic plans that take maximum advantage of such change.

This is no easy task. Indeed, assessing change and formulating appropriate long-range strategic plans is likely to be the single-most important determinant of executive success in direct selling over the next decade. The purpose of this article is to raise questions and provoke discussion about these issues.

Ben M. Enis is Professor of Marketing at the University of Southern California, and a tenured faculty member at three major U.S. universities. Dr. Enis is a member and former National Vice President of the American Marketing Association.

3

The article summarizes a study based on a careful review of relevant literature and data, as well as interviews in person and by telephone with more than thirty direct selling executives and officials of the Direct Selling Association and the Direct Selling Education Foundation. The article also examines major trends on the demand side (changing consumer demographics, lifestyles and buying patterns) and the supply side (the role of the independent sales representative) in the industry and the economy generally. Then possible strategic responses by direct selling executives are suggested. Issues and opportunities in social responsibility are stressed throughout.

THE DEMAND SIDE: THE DIRECT SELLING CUSTOMER

People–markets, consumers–are changing. Fewer and fewer households are of the "traditional" mold: father works, mother keeps house, children at home. The traditional family accounts for less than 18 percent of U.S. households today, and the rate is dropping (*Statistical Abstract*, 1991). Consequently, the traditional direct selling market: home-dwellers, essentially waiting for direct sellers to knock on their doors, is changing. These changes can be documented in terms of demographics, life-styles, and buying habits.

Changing Demographics

Three characteristics of consumer demographics in the U.S. are changing: people are getting older, households are smaller, and income patterns are diverging from the middle class norm.

The median age in the U.S. today is 31 years of age, and it is rising–perhaps to 40 by the year 2000 (*Statistical Abstract*, 1991). Older people generally have more consumption experience, and they have different wants and desires than do younger people. For example, most have opinions about, and many have dealt with, direct selling companies. They know basically how these companies operate, and have rather firm ideas, positive or negative, about them. Thus, the direct seller must more often change attitudes than form them. This is almost always more difficult to accomplish.

U.S. households are shrinking in size. The average number of children living at home is a bit less than 1.1 per household, and is decreasing (*Statistical Abstract*, 1991). Over 1/3 of all children are single-parented (most of these female), and over 22% of all U.S. adults live alone. Consequently, average purchase per household is much less than it used to be–both in amount, and in range of goods and services demanded. For example, if there are no children at home, there may be no demand for children's books or encyclopedias. On the other hand, there are more households in total, and demands require more sophisticated analysis. The childless household, for example may consist of grandparents who may be excellent candidates for books for the grandchildren. The point is that relying upon simple demographic data may produce misleading estimates of sales potential.

Income patterns of U.S. households are diverging from the middle class norm. According to the 1990 census (*Statistical Abstract*, 1991), the proportion of U.S. families in that category $15,000 and $49,999–the middle class–shrank, after adjustment for inflation, from 65.1% in 1970 to 57.1% in 1989. Families with incomes of $50,000 or more–considered the gateway to the upper class–increased from 13% of the population to 19.1% during the 1970-85 period. At the same time, the proportion of families below $15,000 grew from 21.9% to 24.2%.

Moreover, people's perceptions exaggerate the differences. Thus, people increasingly identify with one of two broad income classes: (1) those who see themselves as money-poor and (2) an affluent, but time-poor, perceived segment.

Obviously, the consumption patterns of these groups will be quite different. The money-poor will want satisfactory-quality goods and services at low prices, while the affluent will want high quality goods/services efficiently delivered. Direct selling strategies must be designed and implemented accordingly. Both points are developed in more depth in succeeding sections of this paper.

Changing Lifestyles

As a result of these demographics, and other factors (advancing technology, increasing urbanization and household mobility, changing religious and moral values, to cite just a few), consumers' lifestyles are changing. More specifically, effective understanding of direct selling customers requires a more sophisticated analysis than simple demographics. One potentially useful approach is the Values and Lifestyles (VALS) work of the Stanford Research Institute (Mitchell, 1984).

Based on considerable empirical research, VALS classifies the U.S. population in terms of nine categories

Survivors–Old, intensely poor, fearful, far removed from the cultural mainstream (four percent of the U.S. adult population).

Sustainers–Angry, resentful, street-wise, living on the edge of poverty, involved in the underground economy (7%).

I-Am-Me–Very young, narcissistic, impulsive, exhibitionist (5%).

Socially Conscious–Successful, influential, involved in single-issue politics, seeking simplicity in life (9%).

Belongers–Aging, conventional, content, intensely patriotic, traditional Middle Americans (35%).

Emulators–Young, ambitious, flashy, trying to break into the system (9%).

Achievers–Middle-aged, prosperous, self-assured, the leaders and builders of the American dream (22%).

Integrated–Psychologically mature, tolerant, flexible, able to see "the big picture" (2%).

These classifications provide information beyond simple demographics. The first two categories (Survivors and Sustainers) are "need-driven" that is, their incomes are so low that much consumption is denied them. And yet, they do consume many of the basic items offered by direct sellers, e.g., cosmetics, crafts and games, and they sometimes splurge on luxuries like fancy cars or television sets.

The next three groups (I-Am-Me, Experiential and Socially Conscious) are termed "inner-directed," that is, their values and lifestyles are guided by an internal compass. They may be excellent potential direct selling customers, since they value direct experience (e.g., a home or party demonstration) and seek to simplify their lives (less time spent shopping, perhaps).

The third group (Belongers, Emulators, Achievers) is termed "outer-directed," that is, they are guided by the values and lifestyles of others. Perhaps direct selling companies could best serve these people by identifying opinion leaders for each group, researching their demands carefully, and meeting them fully.

There are other classifications and other studies. The purpose here is not to tout one approach or another, but rather to emphasize the point that the direct selling industry must look carefully and systematically at its customers. Effective marketing strategies can only be founded upon a sophisticated knowledge of consumer behavior.

Changing Buying Habits

Obviously, the changes in customer demographics and lifestyles discussed above (and many others not discussed here) are reflected in changing buying habits. To avoid becoming mired in detail, examples of differences in buying habits are discussed in terms of two demographic segments: the money-poor and the time-poor.

The money-poor segment must budget spending on discretionary or impulse items, which most small-ticket direct sales products are, and certainly must carefully buy big-ticket items. These people are driving the explosive growth in price-oriented mass merchandisers such as Wal-Mart, the nation's largest retailer. At the same time, these people are increasingly wary of being duped by marketers (including direct sellers). Indeed most consumer legislation has been enacted in the name of protecting members of this class of society.

Thus, considerable potential exists for direct sellers who can provide both (1) good value (inexpensive yet not poor quality) goods, and at the same time (2) trustworthy, reliable, caring service. Again, Wal-Mart's national growth is testimony to this. Defining quality goods and caring service, however, will require focused research by specific companies. Different products will be demanded by different VALS groups within the money-poor demographic segment.

The time-poor, on the other hand, seek quality goods and hassle-free service. They demand the best, with little effort required on their part. This segment is growing, both in terms of numbers of households, and in purchasing power per household.

Consequently, the type and number of companies competing to serve this group is large and growing–discount department stores, mass merchandisers, specialty stores, direct mail operations, etc. The challenge here for the direct seller is twofold. First, competition to serve this segment will be intense. Second, traditionally, DS sales representatives have come from the other income/lifestyle class, and therefore might not relate well to the affluent time-poor. More extensive training, and/or recruiting from the affluent class, might be advantageous.

The above comments have focused on changing consumers in the United States, yet direct sellers are increasingly interested in international markets as well. Thus, analyses such as the above would also need to be conducted separately for each market under consideration. Demographic, lifestyle and buying habit characteristics will differ, perhaps markedly, in different countries and markets. In some regions and countries, notably Europe, Japan and Australia, information rivals that available in the U.S. in terms of quantity, accuracy and timeliness. Even in such countries, primary research into consumer behavior is likely to be required. And the need for primary data collection is even more intense in potentially-lucrative, but under-studied societies, such as Indonesia.

Consumers and Social Responsibility

A comment needs to be made about *social responsibility*. Too much has been made of the few companies, sales representatives, and consumers who do not enter into exchange transactions in good faith. Most consumers want to deal honestly and fairly with those who sell to them. Much of the resentment of, and charges of "rip-off" by direct sellers results therefore from lack of understanding of direct selling.

Perhaps time is ripe for an educational campaign about the industry to consumers. There may be a role here for the Direct Selling Association, the Direct Selling Education Foundation, and/or other industry associations. If consumers understand the nature of the industry and the way it operates, perhaps there would be less need for restrictive legislation.

THE SUPPLY SIDE:
THE DIRECT SELLING REPRESENTATIVE

Just like the demand side (consumers), the supply side (the sales representative) of direct selling is changing, too. Following is an analysis of the people, the technology and the capital needed for direct sales representatives.

The Direct Sales Person

The people who consume direct sales products also form the pool from which direct sales people are drawn. Thus, comments above about changing demographics, lifestyles and buying habits are relevant to the recruiting, training, and managing of direct sales representatives.

There are fewer housewives at home, so the proportion of those willing to enter direct selling is lower. Moreover, those who do seek income in this fashion are less and less from the traditional mold–the individual who wants to earn some extra money for a particular purpose by performing essentially a peripheral activity. Of course, some people do fit this mold: housewives, students, retired persons. Direct selling companies should not neglect such people. But the emphasis, for most companies, should shift to recruiting the career-oriented.

The single-parent or single-individual household requires full-time employment providing a steady, dependable income. Even the second income wage earner today has many opportunities for steady, full-time employment, so fewer of them are interested in direct selling as traditionally conceived. They seek careers, or even aspire to entrepreneurship.

Further contributing to the decline in interest in traditional direct selling jobs is the changing nature of remuneration. As noted above, there is a growing segment of low income households. While many are single-parent or one-individual households, a larger number are former blue and white collar workers no longer able to command middle-class incomes. These people want to work, but not as hamburger-flippers or pizza deliverers. They, too, want steady, reliable income potential–a full-time career, not a peripheral activity.

In the author's view, therefore, there are many potential direct salespeople. But they do not want direct selling positions as traditionally conceived by direct selling management. They want, in a word, a *business opportunity*. Direct selling companies should consider their sales representatives as business partners rather than as individuals seeking a bit of loose change. The emphasis should be on helping direct sales representatives to effectively operate their own businesses.

The Technology

Fortunately, the technology to make the above recommendation feasible is becoming available–computers, telecommunications, audio/video tapes and disks, and rapid and reliable package delivery– can be combined into an integrated system for managing the company/sales representative partnership. Each of these components is discussed separately, then their integration is addressed.

Computers. In 1965, eminent science fiction writer Robert A. Heinlein remarked, "There is some new gadget in existence today which will prove to be equally revolutionary [as was the private automobile] . . . You and I both know of this gadget . . . but we don't know which one it is nor what its unexpected effect will be."

Obviously, one such gadget is the desktop or laptop computer. This gadget will make possible the transition from individual sales representative to business operator. Cost and profit analysis, capital budgeting, inventory control, payroll, customer billing, sales forecasts, market analysis, and so on are routinely within its capabilities *provided* that the operator uses it confidently and efficiently. It is essential, therefore, that direct selling companies commit seriously to providing hardware, software, training, and mainframe support for the sales representatives' personal computers.

Telecommunications. Assisting, greatly, in this transition will be telecommunications connections for the computers. Companies can transmit product and price information, shipping schedules, cost-volume-profit standards, selling recommendations, sales training, advertising schedules, etc. to salespeople. They, in turn, can transmit orders, customer/market information, questions about products and prices, product performance by type and by line, etc. The possibilities are endless. Even better use of the simple telephone, for appointment scheduling, order expediting and customer satisfaction review, can improve productivity–especially as cellular technology has made the carphone commonplace.

Audio/Video Tapes and Disks. Another technology developing at breathtaking speed is audio and video tapes and disks. This technology can be used for sales demonstrations to customers and for representative training and information dissemination. Audio tapes or disks containing new product information, selling tips, and company news can be reviewed while driving. Video tapes and disks can be used on portable equipment to enhance sales presentations, and for training purposes.

Package Delivery. The explosive growth of rapid, reliable one or two day small package delivery services means that the sales representative need not hold large inventories of products–tying up home or car space and more importantly, capital. Small inventories of small-ticket items, and direct shipment of big-ticket sales, can result in the same types of savings as manufacturing plants enjoy with "just-in-time" inventory systems. Japanese manufacturers, in particular, have shown that considerable savings can be effected by holding small inventories and relying upon precise, computer-driven ordering systems to maintain schedules and serve customers.

Integrated System. Computers, telecommunications, tapes and disks, and package delivery have literally unlimited potential for improving sales representative productivity. If "high tech" can be combined with "high touch"–quality people well-motivated and managed–the unique advantages of the direct selling approach to retailing can be profitably realized.

The challenge to each company will be to develop and install the total system (hardware, software and operator training) that will best realize that potential. Perhaps there is a role here for the Direct Selling Association to coordinate technological developments and sponsor training seminars, and for the Direct Selling Education Foundation to encourage research into applications problems.

Capital for the Sales Representatives' Business

The good news is that the people and the technology are available for significant improvements in direct selling. The bad news is that the essential human and technological systems discussed above are not cheap. The *business* approach to direct sales representation advocated here requires significant capital.

It is unrealistic to expect that the traditional direct selling representative, or even the new business-seeking type of sales representative, would be able to finance this technology without assistance. The direct selling company, therefore, should be prepared to at least assist the sales representative in determining capital requirements. Ideally (from the sales representative's viewpoint), the company should underwrite the capitalization required.

For many direct selling companies, even the big ones, this ideal may be unrealistic. But capital must be procured–via borrowing secured by the company's debt or equity. Perhaps some direct selling companies could raise sufficient sums in the capital markets. Even if this option were feasible, it is not likely to be the optimal use of the company's capitalization and leverage.

Franchising is one possible answer. Franchising essentially combines the economies of scale of a large operation (quantity buying or manufacture, national advertising, centralized training, standardized accounting records, etc.) with the commitment and motivation of the on-site owner or manager. The *Franchise Handbook* (1991) reported that as of 1990, there were over 360,000 franchisees of more than 2000 different franchisers, exclusive of the traditional auto dealers, gasoline service station operators and soft drink bottlers who founded the franchise movement.

The author believes that independent sales representatives could logically become franchisees of direct selling companies. And with proper planning and marketing, these companies could secure venture capital for a franchising arrangement. To be sure, franchising is not a popular topic among direct selling executives. There are real problems, not least of which is significant information disclosure requirements. Nor would the process be easy to implement for any company. But the issue of capitalization must be addressed. So, franchising should be seriously considered, if the *business* approach to sales representation is to be a realistic option for direct selling.

Socially Responsible Direct Selling Behavior

People, technology and capital can be brought together by the direct selling companies to provide independent direct sales representatives with an attractive career, selling useful products to consumers who will benefit from them. This is the essence of socially responsible behavior.

This approach would strengthen and preserve private enterprise, provide career opportunities in an expanding economy, and serve consumers well. And it could be featured in a dynamic public relations campaign which would enhance the image of the industry.

THE DIRECT SELLING COMPANY

This section focuses on marketing activities and relationships of the company with sales representatives and customers. In short definition, marketing involves (1) finding a need, and (2) filling that need.

Finding a Need: Market Information

Traditionally, direct selling companies have relied for the most part on sales representatives to find customers. Even when advertising produced customer responses, these were seen only as sales leads, to be turned over to the sales representative who had the territorial prerogative. The potential value of that response as market information was not often recognized. Stated more broadly, direct selling companies rarely invested in solid market research.

Even if such lack of investment were justified at one time, it cannot be so today. Direct selling companies should develop or buy systematic, comprehensive data bases on present and potential consumers, and on competition. Information can be obtained from internal records, intelligence, and primary research projects.

Records. The place to start building a data base is with internal records—primarily accounting information. Most companies know how much of each product is sold, and to whom (if they access sales representatives' records). Some can determine cost-volume-profit relationships for each product or product line. Few, however, have data collection and analytical routines which identify customers by demographic, lifestyle or buying habits, or rate competitor strengths and weaknesses. Much of this information is known to the sales representative, or could be collected by him/her, if proper procedures were available.

The company, in short, often knows who bought, but rarely why. Thus, internal accounting information is seldom useful for sales forecasting, new product development, advertising effectiveness, or sales force productivity studies. With sufficient effort and perhaps expert guidance, accounting records can be designed to collect significant customer and competitive information. Direct Selling companies must allocate the resources to bring accounting systems up to this level of information provision.

Intelligence. A second type of market information is intelligence. In the military as opposed to the psychological sense, intelligence refers to the collection of information that is available in the external environment (as opposed to internal records).

Most direct selling executives read widely in the general business and specific direct selling literatures. But few have comprehensive, systematic frameworks for collecting, storing, collating, analyzing, and disseminating what they find. Some of the larger companies have libraries, and subscribe to syndicated services such as the Yankelovich Monitor of the Market Research Corporation of America's consumer purchase panel.

Again, however, experience shows that such information rarely gets into the hands of new product planners, advertising copywriters, or sales trainers. A concerted effort should be made to design and implement an intelligence gathering, storing, analyzing and disseminating system. Such a system would involve periodic structured questioning of executives, sales representatives and outside experts; comprehensive scanning of books, periodicals and government publications; subscriptions to syndicated services; and, most importantly, an organized library to collate, summarize and store the information, and disseminate it to appropriate decision-makers.

Research Projects. The third type of marketing information is that generated by specific research projects. Three general types are focus groups, surveys and experiments.

As most direct selling executives know, a focus group means just that: a small (usually 6-10 people) group who focus discussion on a particular topic. A group of consumers, for example, might be brought together under the leadership of a trained moderator to discuss a company's new product, or an advertising campaign, or sales after service. A group of sales representatives could focus on consumers' perceptions of our product vis-à-vis those of competitors. This technique does not produce scientifically valid data, but is often used at the beginning of the research process to identify issues for more scientific study. Of course, sometimes answers are so clear that they literally cry out, especially to experienced executives observing the group from behind one-way glass or on videotape.

When more scientific information is desired, the most common technique is the survey. Mail, telephone or in-person questioning can generate useful information about many, many topics. The author believes strongly that, just as an executive would not go to court without an attorney, neither should she/he design a survey instrument without expert help. The survey technique, in short, is neither easy nor inexpensive, but provides information valuable in excess of its costs in many cases.

A final research technique is the experiment. Here the information given to the respondent (usually the consumer) is manipulated by the researcher to highlight specific responses. For example, consumers may be shown different advertisements to determine which provokes more responses. Or product features may be varied to assess acceptance. As with surveys, marketing experimentation is a job for experts to do–in conjunction with direct selling executives. The decision maker must be closely involved in the research project if the information is to be of value.

Many small companies simply cannot afford the kind of systematic, comprehensive approach to information procurement advocated here. But such information is needed for effective decision making. Perhaps there is a role here for the Direct Selling Association, or other cooperative information-generating venture among direct selling companies. The Direct Selling Education Foundation could also focus basic and applied research efforts here.

Filling a Need: Marketing Strategy

Marketing strategy is generally developed in two stages: overall goals and resource commitments, and specific programs.

Ideally, marketing objectives are derived from careful marketing research. If information is not available, executives intuitively decide what the target level of sales will be, by product line and/or sales territory. Then the resources (people, capital, information technology, inventory, etc.) necessary to support those objectives are allocated. Often, a company can profit from a systematic and critical review of its objective-setting and resource allocation procedures.

The next step is the development of a specific program for a given product line. The standard grouping of marketing program decision categories is Product, Promotion, Place, and Price–the "4 Ps."

Product. According to the simple but useful scheme developed by the Boston Consulting Group, a product line can be classified in one of four categories: (1) "cash cow"–a mature product enjoying sufficient market acceptance that sales generate revenue in excess of that needed to maintain the desired sales level; the cow therefore can be "milked" of cash flow to fund (2) "question marks" or "wildcats"–new products which hopefully will experience rapid market acceptance, to become (3) "stars"–products still growing in market acceptance, hopefully generating enough revenue to cover their costs: when the growth slows, successful stars become cash cows, generating cash for future question markets. Of course, a product can at any time for many reasons generate less revenue than it needs; unless this is a new product question mark, this product is designated (4) a dog.

This relatively simple-sounding concept is in actuality a powerful framework for marketing program decision-making. While not easy to put into empirical practice, the concept precisely guides thinking about all four types of decisions. New products, for example, must be tested in the marketplace, and require educational promotion to induce consumer trial. Mature products, in contrast, require the development of new features and need only reminder-type promotion. And the concept emphasizes the importance of a balanced "portfolio" of products–cows to provide revenue today, stars to be tomorrow's cows, and wildcats to be tomorrow's stars. Even the small company which has only one product line should consider developing new products–at least variations on its basic line.

Promotion. Ralph Waldo Emerson said–mistakenly–"if you make a better product . . . people will beat a path to your door." Direct sellers have traditionally beat a path to customers' doors. This is no longer sufficient. Promotion today must do more, in terms of both "push" and "pull."

Push-type promotion in direct selling is the work of the sales representative: personal selling to the consumer. For all the reasons outlined above, the direct sales representative today must be a more professional business person. Knocking on doors cold will not generate sufficient business. Telephoning for appointments or even for closing must be used.

Sales representatives may need a wider assortment to sell to justify the expense of the sales call (for some, this may mean representing more than one non-competing company, as industrial sales reps often do). For example, the cookware or Tupperware representative could add a cookbook line, or even a cosmetic or crafts line. Additional outlets, such as mall locations or "parties" held in hotel ball rooms, will need to be evaluated. The latter could become real events, with live entertainment, and/or meals served, and/or product demonstrations via multi-media shows, in addition to sales presentations.

Pull-type promotion includes advertising, both mass and direct mail, and also promotions such as rebate coupons, entries in prize drawings, additional merchandise, etc. Also to be considered as promotional are such things as quantity or seasonal buying discounts, credit terms, etc. Successful push and pull promotion requires integration with product development, distribution and pricing. Some companies do this well while many could profit from systematic review of these disparate elements.

Place. Distribution traditionally has been the sales representative delivering the product ordered to the customer. This procedure provided additional selling time, as well as on-the-spot attention to complaints. But the changing consumer trends discussed in the first section of this paper necessitate careful review of this distribution method.

It is expensive, at least in terms of opportunity costs, for the sales representative to make the delivery trip, even if all goes well. And too often, the customer is not home, or cannot or will not pay at this time. Again, a careful, systematic examination of this part of marketing strategy is recommended. Perhaps package delivery, as discussed above, would be more cost-effective. At the very least, the sales representative should understand the opportunity costs and benefits of this method of distribution.

Direct selling companies should try to alleviate these costs. Telephone order verification from the home office, delivery by rapid package service, and automatic billing via credit card are possibilities. The point is to evaluate separating the promotion effort which the sales representative must perform from the delivery effort. Perhaps an experiment could be designed and executed to determine the costs and benefits for a given company.

Price. The pricing component includes much more than simply selecting a list price for the product. From the supply side, it must not only cover the company's costs, but also allow funding of the sales representative's activities. As noted above, the author believes that direct selling companies should seriously consider a franchising arrangement, or some other means of assisting the sales representative to cover costs. From the demand side, the price must reflect consumers' desires as well as competitors' activities. There is no substitute here for accurate and timely marketing information.

In summary, various aspects of the pricing function must be integrated among themselves, and with other aspects of the marketing program. And this program must be coordinated with the work of the sales representatives. All of this requires a more dedicated and sophisticated effort than most American businesses generally exhibit. Indeed, marketing pundit Philip Kotler maintains that he can count the truly marketing-oriented American companies on one hand. That judgment may be a bit harsh; the good news is that any company can improve its marketing performance. There is ample evidence that such improvement shows up well on the bottom line.

Ethical and Social Considerations

Direct Selling companies can generate considerable goodwill today by paying explicit attention to social responsibility, and of course then claiming credit for so doing. Here are a few examples.

A consumer advocate once posed the following hypothetical situation to the author: "Suppose that consumer research shows that there is a segment of direct selling customers who purchase, but do not use, many products. They are lonely, and are willing to spend money for goods they do not need to secure time for conversation with sales representatives. What should the direct selling company do?" Profits would be maximized by training representatives to load up such customers with products. Is that ethical? How about a program to alleviate loneliness without a purchase obligation? Would such a program subsequently pay for itself in goodwill and later sales? If telecommunications technology succeeds as predicated above, will there be a greater potential role for homebound and/or disabled persons as direct salespeople? Could direct selling companies take positive (as distinguished from court-mandated affirmative) action? And then advertise the success of this program?

The Direct Selling Association Code has earned respect among consumer advocates. Is this success known generally? Could DSA develop a public relations campaign to educate all consumers—and coincidentally increase awareness of its own code?

These are but a few examples of the general point that it is possible to "do well by doing good." The Direct Selling industry should look carefully at opportunities here.

CONCLUSIONS

This report examines managerial issues in direct selling channels today. Major findings focusing on the four major "players" in the industry—customers, sales representatives, companies, and society are summarized. Conclusions and recommendations are offered.

Customers. Direct selling customers are changing—in demographic characteristics, lifestyles, and buying patterns. The direct selling industry must devote significant resources to continuous, systematic study of customers, including internal sales records, market intelligence, and primary research.

Sales Representatives. Major changes are required in relationships between direct selling companies and sales representatives. Many sales representatives today are career oriented; they see themselves as, or aspire to be, entrepreneurs. Companies should consider the representatives as operating on-going independent businesses, rather than as individuals who move into and out of the labor force as circumstances dictate. The *franchise* form would appear to offer significant potential benefits to direct selling companies and independent sales representatives.

Companies. Direct selling companies face increasingly severe competition, not only among themselves, but also from other types of retailers. Government regulation poses both threats and opportunities. And internal performance pressures, from employees and stockholders, are increasingly intense. Direct selling companies should review marketing systems and procedures to become more productive. A comprehensive, systematic approach–termed in the marketing literature a *Marketing Audit* is recommended.

Society. The importance of social responsibility is a theme throughout this article. There is increasing interest in business ethics, consumer satisfaction, and community participation. The direct selling industry should carefully consider ways to perform socially responsible activities and be favorably perceived for so doing by public opinion.

This is an exciting time for those interested in direct selling channels. Many significant managerial challenges and research opportunities are offered throughout the globe by these changing times in direct selling.

REFERENCES

A Bibliography of Direct Selling in the United States: Selected and Annotated (1991), Washington, DC: Direct Selling Educational Foundation.

Celente, Gerald, with Tom Milton (1990). *Trend Tracking: The System to Profit From Today's Trends*. New York: John Wiley & Sons.

Drucker, Peter F. (1969), *The Effective Executive*. New York: Harper & Row.

———— (1985), *Innovation and Entrepreneurship*. New York: Harper & Row, Publishers, Inc.

Day, George S. (1990), *Market Driven Strategy: Processes for Creating Value*: New York: The Free Press.

The Franchise Handbook (1992), ed. M.J. Mc Dermott, Enterprizes Magazine, Summer Issue.

Garreau, Joel (1981), *The Nine Nations of North America*. New York: Avon Books.

Gilder, George F. (1984), *The Spirit of Enterprise*. New York: Simon & Shuster.

Hazlitt, Henry (1946), *Economics in One Lesson*. New York: Harper.

Jones, Constance & The Philip Life Group, Inc. (1987). *The 220 Best Franchises to Buy: The Source Book For Evaluating The Best Franchise Opportunities*. New York: Bantam Books.

Kotler, Philip (1985), *The New Competition*. Englewood Cliffs, NY: Prentice-Hall Inc.

Kotter, John P. (1982), *The General Managers*. New York: The Free Press.

Levitt, Theodore (1983), *The Marketing Imagination*. New York: The Free Press.

Mitchell, Arnold (1983), *The Nine America Lifestyles*. New York: Warner Books, Inc.

Naisbett, John (1984), *Megatrends*. New York: Warner Books, Inc.

Peters, Thomas J. and Nancy Austen (1985), *Passion for Excellence*. New York: Random House.

_____ and Robert H. Waterman, Jr. (1982) *In Search of Excellence*. New York: Harper and Row, Publishers, Inc.

Porter, Michael E. (1980), *Competitive Strategy*. New York: The Free Press.

Spencer, Cheryl (1986), "Computers That Go Home," *Personal Computing*. (October), 160-165.

Stanat, Ruth (1990), *The Intelligent Corporation: Creating A Shared Network For Information and Profit*. New York: Amacom.

Statistical Abstract of the United States 1980 (1980), Washington, D.C.: U.S. Bureau of the Census.

Statistical Abstract of the United States 1986 (1986), Washington, D.C.: U.S. Bureau of the Census.

Statistical Abstract of the United States 1991 (1991), Washington, D.C.: U.S. Bureau of the Census.

Strazewski, Jan (1986), "Families Tune in for Efficiency, Entertainment," *Advertising Age* (January 9), 9-11.

Totty, Michael (1986), "Small Businesses Find Electronic Banking Can Be a Useful Tool in Managing Money," *Wall Street Journal* (July 22), 33.

Tyson, David O. (1986), "Expert Estimates 75,000 Use Video Banking," *American Banker* (January 14), 9.

Wall Street Journal (1986), "Television Trends," (July 18), 23.

Wickham, Penelope, Editor (1988), *Demographic Know-How: Everything Marketers Need To Know About How To Find, Analyze And Use Information About Their Customers*. Ithaca, New York: American Demographics Press.

INTERVIEWS

A very important component of this study was a set of interviews conducted by the author. He spoke, in person or by telephone, with the following direct selling executives, officials and experts, listed below with their affiliations at the time of the interview. Much valuable information was obtained; many of these people gave considerable time and endured numerous questions. Of course, interpretation of the information obtained is the responsibility of the author.

Monty C. Barber
   Executive Vice President/Secretary/General Counsel,
   Mary Kay Cosmetics, Inc.

Richard H. Bell, Chairman of the Board
   Highlights for Children, Inc.

Steven D. Cooper, Vice President & General Counsel
   Electrolux Corporation

Neil M. Ford, Chairman, Marketing Department
   University of Wisconsin

J. Stanley Fredrick, Chairman of the Board
   Cameo Coutures, Inc.

Marlene W. Futterman, Executive Director
   Direct Selling Education Foundation

Robert Grayson, Publisher
   The Journal of Consumer Marketing

Dennis Harmon, Associate Director
   Direct Selling Association

George C. Hescock, Director
   Direct Selling Association

Daniel O. Jensen, President
   Jenkon Data Systems, Inc.

George H. Karlin, President
   The Creative Circle

Robert H. King, President
Consumer Marketing Services, Inc.

Erick J. Laine, President and Chairman of the Board
Alcas Cutlery Corporation-CUTCO

E. Don Lovelace, President
Lady Love Cosmetics, Inc.

Laurence J. Maher, Vice President EB International
Encyclopedia Britannica, Inc.

Paul B. Markovits, Executive Vice President, U.S.
Avon Products, Inc.

Morris L. Mayer, Professor of Marketing
University of Alabama

Patricia Mulcahy, Vice President, Administration
Encyclopedia Britannica, Inc.

Neil H. Offen, President
Direct Selling Association

Donald B. Smith, retired
Avon Products, Inc.

Charles E. Swanson, retired
Encyclopedia Britannica U.S.A.

Thomas R. Wotruba, Professor of Marketing
San Diego State University

Consumer Responses to Direct Selling: Love, Hate ... Buy?

J. Thad Barnowe
David E. McNabb

SUMMARY. This paper describes findings from an investigation of consumers' experiences with and attitudes toward direct selling methods, based upon face-to-face interviews with 491 residents in three Pacific Northwest metropolitan areas. Demographic differences in purchase behavior and in preferences for different selling methods are reported, along with consumers' responses to open-ended questions concerning what they like and dislike about direct selling, and their ideas for improvement of direct selling methods.

Although direct selling is a centuries-old set of practices, and is the bread and butter of a number of successful organizations today, the academic research literature on direct selling is still relatively sparse. In particular, relatively little research has been conducted on consumer responses to direct selling, and what has been done has presented disturbing news about the image of the direct selling industry in general. Two studies commissioned by the Direct Selling Association, conducted by Louis Harris and Associates (1977) and The Nowland Organization

J. Thad Barnowe is Professor of Management, and David E. McNabb is Professor of Marketing in the School of Business Administration at Pacific Lutheran University, Tacoma, WA.

This research was funded by a grant from the Direct Selling Educational Foundation.

The authors wish to thank Marlene Futterman, Executive Director of the Direct Selling Education Foundation, who provided helpful comments and criticism at each stage of instrument development, and the senior marketing and merchandising staff at Jafra Cosmetics, Shaklee, and Discovery Toys, who served as key informants in early stages of instrument development.

(1982), reported that while consumers' personal experiences with direct selling have been generally positive, the image they held of the direct selling industry was negative in a number of respects. According to Louis Harris and Associates (1977: 7), consumers reported that direct selling (especially the use of cold calls) represents an intrusion, and that they are concerned about letting strangers into their homes, being subjected to high sales pressure and the use of misleading and unfair sales tactics, ending up buying products they don't need, and paying an unfair price for products sold direct. According to Nowland (1982), consumers hold generally negative views about the very idea of direct selling, and many perceive that direct salespersons are overly aggressive, unmotivated (substituting transitory contacts for true salesmanship), and capitalize on friendships, or emphasize selling business opportunities and premiums rather than merchandise and delivery.

This study was designed to update and extend the findings of the surveys by Louis Harris and Associates (1977) and the Nowland Organization (1982) concerning consumers' attitudes toward direct selling, and to document direct buying patterns and to profile characteristics of heavy users of direct selling. It addresses in particular the following questions: Who buys products and services offered through direct selling? What kinds of products or services are most frequently purchased? What do consumers appreciate most ("love") about the opportunity to buy through direct selling methods, or about the process of direct selling itself? What do consumers find least attractive ("hate") about direct selling? Of the latter, which aversive aspects of direct selling are most amenable to change by direct selling organizations?

This study sought to answer these questions by randomly sampling, via door to door interviews, consumers' responses to direct selling attempts in three cities in the U. S. Pacific Northwest. For purposes of the study, direct selling was defined as any attempt to sell a product or service made person-to-person away from a regular place of business.

METHOD

Sample

Data were collected through face-to-face interviews in 491 households in three Pacific Northwest major metropolitan areas:

Seattle/Tacoma (165), Spokane (150), and Portland (176). In each metropolitan area, care was taken to ensure that lower, middle, and upper income neighborhoods would by sample by first reviewing 1980 census income data and then scouting each census tract in advance of data collection. Most of the interviewing was completed on weekends, to ensure that large numbers of household members would be at home, and to increase the number of men among the survey's respondents. Table 1 shows profiles of respondent characteristics obtained through the above stratified quota sampling procedures.

Survey Instrument

A structured-disguised survey instrument was prepared, based in large part upon interviews with key informants familiar with direct selling, including senior marketing and merchandising staff at a number of direct selling corporations. The instrument assessed the following:

Preferences for alternative selling methods. Respondents described their purchase behaviors with respect to alternative selling methods (including direct selling methods, mail order, telephone solicitation, and buying services), and their preferences for those methods.

Direct selling purchase behavior. Respondents were asked to enumerate products or services they had purchased in the last three years, which had been sold face to face away from a regular place of business. They were also asked to indicate whether they had experienced any attempts at direct selling, whether they made any purchase or not, including experiences with direct selling attempts in the workplace.

Reactions to direct selling. Eleven questions assessed respondents' reactions to the quality of goods and services sold through direct selling, and their characterizations of personalized attention, price, opportunity to ask questions, convenience, warranty and service provisions, opportunity to obtain additional product or replacement parts, and ability to try a product to see it demonstrated associated with direct selling. Respondents also described advantages, disadvantages, and improvements they would like to see in the way products and services are sold through direct methods.

Demographics included sex and ethnicity of respondent; house-

Table 1

Sample Demographic Characteristics

Respondent characteristics (%)		Household characteristics (%)	
Sex		Size:	
Male	42.0	One person	22.5
Female	58.0	Two persons	32.0
Ethnicity		Three persons	21.3
White	88.8	Four persons	12.7
African-American	7.6	Five persons	6.8
Hispanic	1.9	Six or more	4.7
Asian	1.5	Children under age 18:	
Other	.2	No children	65.8
Education		One or more	34.2
Less than 8th grade	.2	Seniors age 60+:	
Some high school	6.4	No seniors	80.0
High school grad/GED	29.6	One or more	20.0
Some college	31.9	Income:	
College grad	23.7	Under $15,000	15.3
Postgrad work/degree	8.2	$15,000-$25,000	27.8
Marital status		$25,000-$40,000	33.0
Single	23.2	Over $40,000	24.0
Married	53.7	Type of residence:	
Divorced	10.0	Private house	85.5
Separated	6.4	Duplex	6.4
Widowed	6.8	Apartment	6.4
Age		Mobile home	1.0
19 or younger	2.3	Room	.6
20-29	23.2	Owned or rented:	
30-39	22.4	Owned	68.3
40-49	19.2	Rented	31.7
50-59	14.2	Length of residency:	
60-69	13.2	Under 1 year	13.2
70 or older	5.4	1-5 years	34.6
Employment status		6-10n years	15.2
Employed full time	61.0	11-20 years	16.7
Less than full time	11.0	Over 20 years	20.4
Unemployed/looking	2.1		
Retired	13.3		
Student/homemaker/other	12.6		

hold size and composition; age, marital status, education, occupation and employment status of head of household; family income; and length of residency.

Demographic differences in preferences for alternative selling methods, direct selling purchase behavior, and reactions to direct selling were analyzed using analysis of variance with *a posteriori* comparisons, and are reported within each topical section below.

RESULTS

Consumers' Preferences for Selling Methods

When asked about the extent to which they like to or prefer to buy products or services through various selling methods, respondents indicated a strong preference for shopping at retail stores or a regular place of business. As shown in the first four columns of Table 2, 97 percent liked (including "very much liked") retail store shopping; 83 percent liked mail order catalog shopping; and 57 per cent liked responding to mailed offers or advertisements. Three direct selling methods received a relatively favorable response: just over half of the study's sample liked attending parties in another's home, and more than one third liked appointments in their own home or parties in their home. Selling through parties in the workplace was comparatively unpopular (with just under one quarter of the sample responding favorably), and door to door sales along with unsolicited telephone sales received a very unfavorable response.

Differences in preferences for direct selling methods were examined through one-way analysis of variance with modified least-squares *a posteriori* tests. Women held significantly more favorable preferences than men for door to door sales and for parties, whether in their own home, in another's home, or at work. Respondents under age 30 held more favorable preferences for door to door sales than those over age 30. Respondents with a high school education and those with some college preferred parties at another's home more than those with postgraduate education; respondents with some college preferred parties at work more than did college gradu-

Table 2

Preferences for and Purchases through Different Selling Methods

| Method | Preferences[a] | | | | Purchases |
	Very much like	Like	Dislike	Strongly dislike	Per cent reporting
Retail store shopping	51.6%	45.5%	2.1%	0.0%	b
Mailed catalogs	18.1	65.4	11.0	3.3	79.6
Buying service	7.0	43.4	23.6	9.6	31.2
Mailed offers/advertisements	3.3	53.8	27.4	11.0	58.4
Toll-free telephone numbers	8.5	38.1	29.6	13.5	b
Party in other's home	6.4	44.3	29.4	14.8	
Appointments at home	3.3	40.8	29.9	21.3	
Party in own home	4.2	32.1	37.1	23.6	
Cable TV shopping channel	1.3	15.4	30.3	25.9	8.7
Party at workplace	1.7	22.6	43.8	25.1	
Door to door sales	0.2	11.6	42.3	41.3	
Unsolicited telephone calls	0.2	9.5	36.2	52.8	32.4
Direct selling (combined)					58.5

Note: Italics indicate direct selling methods.
[a] Listed in order by mean score.
[b] Purchase behavior not assessed.

ates. Those who had lived in their residence from six to ten years preferred parties in another's home more than did those who had lived in their residence more than twenty years.

Direct Selling Events and Purchases

Although direct selling methods were not the most preferred methods of selling for respondents in this study (nor, except for door to door sales, the least preferred), were the methods nonetheless effective? An affirmative answer is suggested by two observations. First, a vast majority of this study's 491 respondents (91.9%) had experienced a direct selling encounter in which someone had tried to sell to them door to door, in their own home, at a party in someone else's home, or elsewhere away from a regular place of retail business. Second, as shown in the far right column of Table 2, more than half of the respondents (58.5%) indicated that on one or more occasions during the past three years they or someone in their household had purchased a product or service sold directly. This means that nearly two-thirds (65.1%) of the households that had experienced at least one direct sales effort in the last three years had made at least one purchase. Direct selling methods thus appear to be very competitive with other approaches to selling (retail shopping excluded).

Several statistically significant differences were observed in the demographic characteristics of subjects who made purchases of goods or services through direct selling events, and those who did not. Women made significantly more purchases than men (65.8% versus 47.7%; chi-square = 14.78, df = 1, p < .0001). Household size was positively associated with purchase behavior: 64.9% of households with three or more persons had made purchases through direct selling, compared to 53.4% of households with two or fewer persons (chi-square = 8.30, df = 3, p = .04). Households with one or more children under age 18 also made significantly more purchases: 67.9%, compared to 53.6% of households without children (chi-square = 8.72, df = 1, p = .003). Although the difference was statistically significant only at the .12 level, younger respondents tended to report making direct selling purchases more often than older respondents: 63.8% of respondents under age 40, compared to 53.4% of respondents over age 40, reported purchases in the past three years (chi-square = 5.76, df = 3).

There were no significant differences in buying through direct selling as a function of occupation, income, whether a household was owned or rented, length of residency, ethnicity of respondent, whether seniors were present, marital status, education, or employment status.

Products/Services Purchased Through Direct Selling

Table 3 lists, in rank tiers, the products and services most frequently purchased through direct selling. Food, cosmetics, kitchen and home cleaning products, books and magazines, items of clothing, interior decorations, and raffle tickets occupy the upper tiers of products which were purchased; however, a very large variety of products and services received at least one mention. The diversity

Table 3

Most Frequently Purchased Products or Services

Rank tier	Product/Service	Per cent mentioning
1	Food products	22.7%
2	Cosmetics	14.6
3	Kitchen items	11.7
4	Books/magazines	10.1
5	Housecleaning products	7.4
6	Clothing items	6.3
	Interior decorations	6.3
	Raffle tickets	6.3
7	Christmas items	3.1
8	Lightbulbs	2.3
9	Crystal	2.2
10	Recreational products	2.0
11	Vacuum cleaners	1.8
12	Vitamins	1.6
13	Records/tapes	1.1
14	Insurance	0.9
15	Ceramics	0.7
	Plants	0.7
	Tools	0.7
16	Jewelry	0.5
	Roofing	0.5
17	Chimney cleaning service	0.4
	Computer software	0.4
	Hair products	0.4
	Home security equipment	0.4
	Shoes	0.4
18	Automotive products	0.2
	Calendars	0.2
	Health care products	0.2
	Pictures	0.2
	Sheets/bedding	0.2
	Stationery	0.2
	Miscellaneous (e.g., key chains)	0.2

of products and services actually sold, together with reports of the very large number of direct selling attempts respondents had encountered, suggest a voluminous amount of direct selling activity by a large number of companies (information about specific companies is reported by McNabb and Barnowe, 1988).

Perceived Attributes of Direct Selling

Table 4 reports responses to a structured set of questions concerning attributes of direct selling. Table 5 reports content-coded responses to open-ended questions concerning advantages and disadvantages associated with purchasing goods and services sold through direct methods.

The most favorably perceived attributes of direct selling–attributes about which there was more agreement than disagreement–were characteristics of the transaction between buyer and seller, rather than characteristics of the products or services, price, or after-sales issues. Ability to try a product or see it demonstrated, to interact with the seller, and receive personalized attention were valued by more than half of the study's respondents. Slightly more than half disagreed with the proposition that the quality of goods or services sold direct was better than that for sales at a regular place of business. A solid majority held unfavorable perceptions about follow-up service, warranty protection, price, and even the conve-

Table 4

Perceived Favorable Attributes of Direct Selling

Attribute	Strongly Agree	Agree	Disagree	Strongly Disagree
Ability to try product or have it demonstrated	9.3%	61.3%	20.7%	5.2%
Chance to talk with/ask questions of seller	10.3	55.6	22.7	7.1
Personalized attention	9.4	50.5	25.9	7.6
Quality of products/services	2.0	42.6	32.7	13.3
Convenience	2.4	29.7	43.4	17.5
Price	3.1	23.1	44.9	21.3
Warranty and service	1.9	21.4	40.7	22.2
Ease in getting additional products/replacement parts	2.6	20.3	41.1	24.4

Note: Listed in order by mean score. Percentages indicate agreement-disagreement with the proposition that direct selling is as good as or better than buying at a store or regular place of business, in each respect that is listed.

Table 5

Advantages and Disadvantages of Direct Selling (Open-ended Responses)

Attribute	Per cent
Advantages:	
Convenience	26.8%
Ability to shop at home	17.8
Ability to ask questions, try products	14.1
Only available way to shop	9.4
Chance to meet people	7.5
Personal attention	7.0
Favorable deals	6.1
Good selection	4.2
Contribute to a good cause	2.8
Easier to talk with salesperson	1.4
Better service	1.4
Incentives	0.9
Price comparisons	0.5
Disadvantages:	
Salespersons are too pushy	30.1%
Inconvenient	20.3
Salespersons are untrustworthy	13.4
No place to take problems	6.1
Poor quality of products/services	5.6
Unnecessary products	3.1
Inexperienced salespersons	3.1
Lack of choice	2.8
No follow-up	2.5
No warranty	1.9
Expensive	1.9
Feel obligated to buy	1.7
Other initiates (no control)	1.7
Do not receive product	1.4
Unable to comparison shop	1.1
Not enough information	1.1
Product not readily available	0.6
Hard to get service	0.3
Long catalogs are shown	0.3
Hate religious groups	0.3

nience of direct selling transactions, in comparison with buying at a regular place of business.

Analysis of perceived advantages and disadvantages of direct selling from open-ended responses (which were solicited prior to responses to structured questions) suggests a larger variety of attractions and aversions. Several of the perceived advantages of direct selling (Table 5) reinforce the findings shown in Table 4. The three most frequently mentioned reflect aspects of convenience in the transaction itself. For a smaller number of respondents, direct selling may meet social needs. Other attractions were more idiosyncratic, though less frequent; ability to contribute to a good cause; ability to talk more comfortably with the salesperson; favorable selection and favorable deals. Nearly one in ten respondents indicated that direct selling was the only available way for them to shop.

Disadvantages which were volunteered most frequently centered principally upon the nature and behavior of salespersons. Salespersons were criticized as being too pushy and untrustworthy, or (for fewer respondents) inexperienced. Although convenience was listed by some respondents as an advantage, for others direct selling clearly poses an inconvenience, possibly reflecting the intrusiveness of the direct selling encounter. Many of the other concerns expressed had to do with product quality and after-sale experience, but these were reported by relatively few respondents.

Several demographic differences in attitudes toward direct selling were observed. Women held significantly more favorable perceptions than men concerning the quality of goods and services offered through direct selling, the personalized attention one receives, ability to ask questions of the vendor, warranty and service that is available, ability to obtain additional goods or services later, and the opportunity to try out a product or service. Respondents who worked part time held more favorable attitudes concerning the personalized attention received through direct selling, compared to full-time employees. Respondents from three-person households held more favorable attitudes concerning product quality, price, and the convenience of shopping through direct selling, compared to those from one or two-person households.

Consumers' Suggestions for Improvements in Direct Selling

The improvements which respondents volunteered for making direct selling more attractive are listed in Table 6. Many of those most frequently mentioned relate to the timing and nature of the direct selling transaction itself. Suggestions for making appointments and not coming to one's house may reflect values for privacy and control over initiation of encounters which may be common in American society. Other suggestions reinforce the sense of annoyance and frustration that respondents have with direct selling encounters reflected in the findings reported above, especially regarding the competence and professionalism of salespersons (their training, legitimacy, and pushiness), product quality and selection, and follow-on service and protections.

Table 6

Desired Improvements in Direct Selling (Open-ended Responses)

Improvement	Per cent
Make appointments	21.7%
Better trained salespersons	11.5
Better quality products	10.1
Less pushy salespersons	9.2
Have legitimate salespersons	6.9
Stop coming to house	5.5
Better advertising	5.1
Telephone after sale	4.6
More variety/choice	4.6
Sell familiar products	3.7
Have products available	2.8
Offer warranties	2.8
Offer more flexible price	2.8
Make more convenient	2.3
Provide better product descriptions	1.8
Offer better guarantee	1.4
Come more often	1.4
Do not telephone	0.9
Make visits shorter	0.5
Offer handcrafted items	0.5

DISCUSSION

Some of the findings reported above serve chiefly to reinforce what is known from industry statistics and from previous research about direct selling: that attempts at direct selling reach a very large proportion of households; that food products, cosmetics, cooking and cleaning items and books and magazines are the leading products bought through direct selling; and that consumers find some aspects of direct selling, compared to other forms of shopping and purchasing, annoying or aversive. Other findings suggest several new criticisms of direct selling, but also indicate areas in which direct sellers might attempt to enhance favorable consumer perceptions.

This study supports industry claims that a very high proportion of households experience direct selling attempts (e.g., Gates, 1988). More of this study's households (92%) had experienced direct selling attempts in the past three years than were reported in the Harris (1977) survey for a five-year period (88%). This study's findings also reinforce previous studies which have indicated that women make more purchases through direct selling than do men.

As was the case in earlier studies by Harris and Associates (1977) and the Nowland Organization (1982), consumers in this study complained about pushy, untrustworthy salespersons and about the inconvenience (intrusiveness) of some direct selling encounters. More than in the previous studies, consumers in this study criticized the poor quality of products and services, and of follow-up service, including warranties and recourse in event of problems.

On the positive side, direct selling provides, for some consumers, a set of strong attractions: personalized attention in the convenience of one's own or another's home, the chance to ask questions, and the chance to try products or have them personally demonstrated. For some of this study's respondents, direct selling provided a welcome opportunity for social interaction, or was simply the only available way for them to shop.

One challenge for the direct selling industry is to develop more and better ways to capitalize on these perceived advantages, while reducing the perceived downside of direct selling experiences. The question for this image-conscious industry has always been *how* to do so. This study's respondents have, through their open-ended responses to questions about how to improve direct selling, provided potentially useful practical advice to the direct selling industry regarding the training and development of salespersons and about the process of direct selling itself. Their message: Provide more professional training for direct salespersons so that they manage the seller-buyer relationship more successfully. Direct salespersons should be more knowledgeable, less pushy, and less intrusive; they should provide better follow-up service, schedule appointments in advance, and offer quality, varieties, warranties, and a greater degree of price flexibility.

This admittedly is difficult advice for an industry which to date has relied heavily on an "independent contractor" approach to staffing (i.e., direct salespersons are often not employees of companies for whom they sell). A stronger role in training and professional development of direct salespersons requires much greater attention to human resource management, a potentially costly change in strategy for some direct selling companies which have until now relied upon relatively cursory training for their sales force. Biggart (1989) quotes an executive from Electrolux, one company which has maintained and trained its own salesforce, as saying that it would be too costly today to start a direct selling operation that relied upon an employee workforce rather than independent contractors.

One answer may be to find middle ground between a fully professionalized, employee-based mode of operation and the flexible and nonbureaucratic but loose and inefficient system of independent workers which many companies have relied upon for years. Some companies have already begun to change their approach. Gates (1988), Markovits (1988), and Sloan (1991) recount the approach Avon has taken to provide a higher level of assistance to its direct salespersons, to learn from the marketplace, and to revitalize its operations.

Perhaps there is much to learn also from some of the more successful direct sellers which have developed a strong organizational culture and have capitalized on that culture as a means of motivation and control. Biggart (1989) describes the role of charisma at Mary Kay cosmetics and other direct sellers in exercising a type of "clan control" over the professional behavior not only of direct employees but also of independent contractor-salespersons.

How urgently direct selling organizations need to explore such changes depends on the behavior of consumers as the country climbs out of the recession of the early 1990s. How precarious is consumers' willingness to purchase through direct selling methods, in the current economy? Will the balance between what consumers find attractive about direct selling and what consumers find unattractive or aversive about direct selling remain stable, or will attractions or aversions become more prominent in consumers' eyes? Are darker times ahead, or can the direct selling industry successfully emphasize the positive and diminish what consumers see as negative aspects of direct selling?

Improving the image of the direct selling industry remains a challenge, especially in light of two developments: First, there are signs that the industry is plateauing at approximately $9 billion in total sales (Lumpkin et al., 1989). Second, direct sellers continue to experience difficulties in recruiting and retaining direct salespersons as women, who traditionally have dominated the industry's salesforces, increasingly enter more conventional occupations.

Our advice for now is: Listen to the marketplace by maintaining ongoing programs of research. The best ideas for meeting consumers' needs often come from consumers themselves.

REFERENCES

Direct Selling Education Foundation. (1991). *Bibliography on Direct Selling in the United States*. (1991). Washington: Direct Selling Education Foundation.

Biggart, N. W. (1989). *Charismatic Capitalism*. Chicago: University of Chicago.

Darian, Jean C. (1987). In-home shopping: Are there consumer segments? *Journal of Retailing*, 63 (Summer), 163-186.

Gates, M. (1988). Direct sales. *Incentive* (September), 98-104.

Louis Harris Associates. (1977). *Highlights of a comprehensive survey of the direct selling industry*. Washington, D.C.: Direct Selling Association.

Lumpkin, J. R., Caballero, M. J., & Chonko, L. B. (1989). *Direct marketing, direct selling, and the mature customer*. Westport, CT: Quorum.

Markovits, P. (1988). Direct selling is alive and well. *Sales and Marketing Management, 140* (10), 76-78.

McNabb, D. E., & Barnowe, J. T. (1988). *The in-home shopper: Segmenting the direct selling market.* Research Project Final Report for the Direct Selling Education Foundation, Pacific Lutheran University.

Nowland Organization, Inc. (1982). *Consumer experiences and attitudes with respect to direct selling.* Washington, D.C.: Direct Selling Association.

Sloan, P. (1991). Avon is calling on new tactics, FCB. *Advertising Age, 62* (1), pp. 3, 41.

Motivation to Become a Direct Salesperson and Its Relationship with Work Outcomes

Thomas R. Wotruba
Pradeep K. Tyagi

SUMMARY. Salespeople working for direct selling firms have varying reasons for taking on this selling job. Twenty-six possible job characteristics that define work motivations were studied, and were found to group into five work motivation patterns. Three of these patterns related significantly with a variety of work outcomes, such as organizational commitment, job satisfaction, performance, and turnover. Such information is useful to guide management in recruiting salespeople with high priority for those work motivations that relate to desirable work outcomes. Researchers may also benefit by including work motivations as a moderating variable in future studies of turnover and other work outcomes.

INTRODUCTION

Direct selling (DS) companies provide job opportunities for people with a wide range of backgrounds and characteristics. A recent report noted that more than $8 billion in annual sales is produced by more than 5 million Americans who sell for these firms, though salesperson turnover in a typical DS firm often exceeds 100% per year (Biggart 1989). A recent summary of studies describing the characteristics of DS salespeople concluded that "direct salespeo-

Thomas R. Wotruba and Pradeep K. Tyagi are Professors of Marketing, College of Business, San Diego State University, San Diego, CA 92182.

The authors thank the Direct Selling Education Foundation for support of the research on which this article is based.

ple are found in all education levels, occupational groups, income levels, and household sizes" (Wotruba 1992), suggesting that DS jobs are accessible to a broad diversity of people regardless of prior business experience or specific qualifications as customarily used by employers to screen prospective jobholders. Direct selling salespeople are, with rare exception, independent agents, and many are part-time workers who tailor their DS efforts to dovetail with family and other responsibilities. Many work either part time or full time for another employer in addition to their DS company (Wotruba 1990b).

The flexibility of DS jobs and their easy accessibility can make these positions attractive to people with a variety of work motivations. Thus, some might take on a DS job to earn income while others might view it as a means of building self-esteem, making friends, proving one's entrepreneurial skills, or simply learning about the business world. In turn, persons with different work motivations might seek correspondingly different rewards or work outcomes. An income-seeker might differ markedly from a friendship-seeker in terms of job effort, sales productivity, and ultimately in contribution to achieving the DS firm's goals and objectives as a business organization.

FOCUS OF THIS STUDY

This study is an exploratory attempt to identify the various work motivations important to persons taking on DS sales jobs. Once these motivations are identified, an attempt is made to determine whether differences in work motivations correspond with differences in work outcomes desired by management such as commitment, performance, job satisfaction, and propensity to stay or quit (turnover). Any such relationships found could be useful to management in DS firms in determining what work motivation appeals to use in recruiting salespeople. In addition, management might consider providing programs or developing policies aimed particularly at strengthening the commitment, performance, satisfaction, and tenure of those persons whose work motivations typically lead to less favorable work outcomes.

RESEARCH QUESTIONS

Two specific research questions will be addressed in this exploratory study:

1. Are there different and identifiable work motivations which describe why people become DS salespeople?

If the answer to question 1 is yes, then:

2. Are particular work motivations for joining DS sales forces associated with corresponding differences in organizational commitment, job satisfaction, performance, and turnover?

Question 1 was explored a number of years ago within a broader study carried out for the Direct Selling Association (Harris 1977). At that time, the study concluded that the four top reasons why people become DS salespeople included (1) "being independent and working hard when I want to"; (2) "a good way to supplement my family income or make a little extra money for myself"; (3) "I enjoy selling"; and (4) "the idea that the harder I work the more money I could make." These were the most popular responses given by all DS salespeople in general, however, rather than identifying distinct groupings of motivations that apply to different groups of salespeople.

No other studies of work motivations have been reported specifically within the occupational context of direct selling, though some studies have dealt with related questions. For instance, Thistlethwaite et al. (1985) surveyed residents of McDonough County, Illinois to determine their involvement in direct selling, and categorized the respondents into four groups: presently active as direct sellers; formerly active as direct sellers; recruited (unsuccessfully) to be a direct seller; and never approached to be in direct selling. Those not currently DS salespeople were asked what would influence them to take a DS sales position, and the answer categories most often occurring included the following:

(1) if I lost my present job and no other job were available; (2) sheer desperation, starvation, irreversible poverty; (3) financial need; (4) if I had the time; and (5) if it was with the right company or right product. Those currently in direct selling were not asked in this study for the reasons why they took that position, however. More recently, Wotruba and Tyagi (1991) measured the met expectations of DS salespeople on a large number of job characteristics, and identified four underlying dimensions from these characteristics including: (1) outcomes and rewards; (2) interpersonal relations; (3) conditions of work participation; and (4) job challenges and demands. This study did not address the importance of those characteristics or underlying dimensions as work motivations, however.

Question 2 involves work outcomes specified as organizational commitment, job satisfaction, performance, and turnover. A turnover model for direct selling incorporating these and other variables was devised by Wotruba, Sciglimpaglia, and Tyagi (1987), though a full test of all the linkages in that model has not been reported. Some of these outcome variables have been assessed in various empirical studies of DS salespeople, however, including a comparison of part-time versus full-time salespeople on satisfaction, performance, and turnover (Wotruba 1990b), a study of the impact of job image on these same three variables (Wotruba 1990a), and the relationship of goal-setting to performance and turnover (Wotruba 1989). Though work motivation was not a part of any of these studies, significant relationships were found among these variables, such as positive associations between job satisfaction and job image, and negative associations between performance and turnover. Whether these relationships would hold for all DS salesperson groups regardless of work motivations was not determined.

Organizational commitment has not previously been examined within the context of direct selling. A strong argument can be made for investigating organizational commitment as a factor affecting sales force behavior, however (Chonko 1986), and this variable has been included in various sales force studies involving retail salespeople (Still 1983), industrial salespeople (Ingram, Lee, and Skinner 1989), and detail salespeople in one consumer goods manufacturing firm (Johnston et al. 1987; Sager and Johnston 1989). In none of these cases, however, was the impact of organizational commitment related to work motivations.

METHOD

Sample and Data Collection. Names and addresses of salespeople from all sections of the U.S. were provided by four participating DS companies: Mary Kay Cosmetics, Saladmaster, Tupperware, and United Consumers Club. A total of 1,600 questionnaires with postage-paid return envelopes were mailed, generating responses from 491 (31% response rate). The average respondent held a DS sales position for about eight months, 85% were female, 62% were married, the median age was 27 and the median household total income was about $27,000.

Variables. Work motivations were measured with a list of 26 job characteristics similar in nature to the list used by Wotruba and Tyagi (1991) in their study of met expectations. Respondents were asked to rate "how important to you personally" is each of the characteristics on the list (see Table 1) using a seven-point scale anchored from "extremely important" to "not important." A factor analysis was employed to group these 26 items into five work motivation patterns, as discussed in the next section, and these results are shown in Table 2.

Organizational commitment was measured using the fifteen-item Organizational Commitment Questionnaire (OCQ) developed by Porter et al. (1974). All the studies cited above (Still 1983; Ingram, Lee, and Skinner 1989; Johnston et al. 1987; Sager and Johnston 1989) employed this same measure. In the present study each item was rated on a seven-point scale anchored by "strongly agree" to "strongly disagree."

Job satisfaction was measured using ten items from the job satisfaction subscales of the Job Diagnostic Survey (JDS) developed by Hackman and Oldham (1974, 1975). The JDS subscales have been used successfully to measure job satisfaction in a variety of studies including some specifically in a sales setting (Becherer, Morgan, and Richard 1982; Tyagi 1985). The ten items involved seven-point rating scales ranging from "extremely dissatisfied" to "extremely satisfied."

Table 1. Mean Importance Ratings of Job Characteristics Used to Measure Work Motivations

Job Characteristics	Importance Ratings	
	Mean	S.D.
1. Working for a company with which I am proud to be associated.	6.31	1.00
2. The job will provide me with feelings of worthwhile accomplishment.	6.20	1.00
3. The job supplies an opportunity for professional growth.	6.16	1.08
4. The job offers the work hours I want.	6.06	1.33
5. A job which provides me with feelings of self-fulfillment.	6.04	1.15
6. The job provides an opportunity for a high level of income.	6.00	1.15
7. Job success will relate directly to my initiative.	5.93	1.18
8. Work in which there is freedom to do the job as I wish.	5.93	1.27
9. Work which gives me a chance to be creative and innovative.	5.92	1.15
10. The job should provide advancement opportunities within the company.	5.92	1.34
11. A job in which success depends greatly on individual effort.	5.88	1.06
12. Opportunity to show that I can handle job responsibilities.	5.81	1.47
13. The work makes use of the skills I have.	5.77	1.23
14. Earnings from my work will be reasonably predictable.	5.73	1.21

15.	Support from supervisors will be available.	5.73	1.39
16.	Work which helps increase my self-esteem.	5.64	1.44
17.	Work which gives me an opportunity to make friends.	5.60	1.41
18.	Receiving attention and appreciation from supervisors.	5.41	1.48
19.	Specific opportunities to develop my selling skills.	5.36	1.39
20.	Gaining the respect of my fellow salespersons for my performance.	5.26	1.58
21.	Opportunity to earn special awards or recognition for good performance.	5.15	1.54
22.	The opportunity to work closely with others on a team.	4.96	1.64
23.	A job in which rejection by prospects is minimal.	4.86	1.62
24.	The job involves selling a product which is highly competitive.	4.83	1.98
25.	A job with high prestige in the eyes of my family and friends.	4.31	1.80
26.	The opportunity to go to sales conventions.	3.28	1.86

Note: The mean scores are calculated from a 7-point scale in which 1 = not important and 7 = extremely important.

Table 2. Factor Analysis of Job Characteristics to Determine
Work Motivation Patterns

Job Characteristics [a]	Loadings on Factor [b]				
	1	2	3	4	5
21. Earn special awards or recognition	.70	.30	.15	.07	.09
19. Develop selling skills	.67	.34	.08	.18	-.01
26. Go to conventions	.66	.14	.28	.06	.03
20. Gaining respect of salespersons	.61	.19	.41	.16	.11
24. Selling highly competitive product	.60	.02	.09	.16	.30
17. Opportunity to make friends	.51	.01	.08	.27	.23
22. Work with others on a team	.51	.09	.42	.16	.04
1. Proud company association	.41	.22	.09	.29	-.01
10. Advancement opportunities	.16	.77	.11	.13	.01
6. Opportunity for high income	.11	.74	.12	.11	.18
3. Professional growth	.16	.72	.22	.22	-.17
11. Success depends on effort	.38	.50	-.08	.31	.12
14. Earnings will be predictable	-.18	.46	.44	.10	.45
7. Success relates to initiative	.18	.42	.18	.15	.07
15. Support from supervisors	.20	.09	.76	.05	.06
18. Appreciation from supervisors	.29	.21	.71	.10	.01
12. Show I can handle responsibilities	.03	.17	.65	.23	-.09
25. Job with high prestige	.38	.06	.47	.20	.07
5. Feelings of self-fulfillment	.28	.11	.17	.79	-.04
2. Feelings of accomplishment	.10	.26	.20	.68	.01
16. Increase my self-esteem	.34	.02	.35	.66	.01
13. Job uses skills I have	.03	.23	.09	.56	.18
9. Can be creative and innovative	.29	.35	-.06	.51	.08
4. Offers work hours I want	.06	.12	-.01	-.06	.80
8. Freedom to do the job as I wish	.36	-.01	-.11	.15	.60
23. Job with minimal rejection	.34	-.03	.37	.16	.48

[a] The number for each characteristic corresponds to the numbers in
Table 1 with the more complete descriptions.

[b] Descriptors assigned to each factor are: Factor 1, social
recognition and organizational identification; Factor 2, income
and career growth; Factor 3, attention and approval; Factor 4,
personal fulfillment and job challenge; Factor 5, autonomy and
control. The items assigned to each factor are indicated by
underlined loadings.

Performance was measured with seven self-rated items modeled after the performance measurement scale by Behrman and Perreault (1982). In the current study, however, some slight modifications were made in the items to reflect more precisely the nature of the direct selling job. These changes resulted from discussions with executives in the sponsoring firms as well as two focus groups of direct salespeople completed prior to the development of the questionnaire. Based on a review of self-evaluation literature (Mabe and West 1982), respondents were promised anonymity and asked to rate their performance rather than their ability via this instruction: "How satisfied are you with the results you are achieving up to today on each of these seven activities": planning and goal setting, locating new potential customers, sales presentations and demonstrations, recruiting new salespersons, meeting with supervisors, follow-up after the sale, and administration. Five-point scales were used, anchored by "completely satisfied" and "not at all satisfied," with intermediate positions labeled as "only slightly satisfied," "somewhat satisfied," and "mostly satisfied."

It should be noted that self-appraisals were used because the firms involved do not prepare any separate performance appraisals of their salespeople. Further, any specific performance result measure, such as sales volume, would be awkward to use for two reasons. First, different DS salespeople spend varying amounts of time in this job, with some being part-time and others full-time. Second, the underlying rationale for this study is that not all DS salespeople have similar work motivations, such as to seek large financial rewards by maximizing sales volume. For both reasons, sales volume or commissions earned would not be valid measures for comparing performance success among these salespeople.

Turnover was measured with a single scale incorporating both quitting and intentions to quit, so that answers could be obtained from respondents who had already quit and others who were still active but in various stages of intending to quit. The scale had six positions as follows: (1) I have never thought about quitting; (2) I seldom think about quitting; (3) I sometimes think about quitting; (4) I frequently think about quitting; (5) I am just about ready to quit; (6) I am no longer active on the job. A cover letter accompanying the questionnaire urged everyone to respond even if they had become inactive in direct selling, and 34% of the respondents placed themselves in category 6.

ANALYSIS AND RESULTS

To assess the internal consistency of the measures used in the research, Cronbach alpha reliability coefficients were calculated for all the criterion variables and predictor variables resulting from the factor analysis. Reliability estimates for criterion variables varied from .83 for job performance to .95 for job satisfaction. For predictor variables, alpha values ranged between .50 and .83. Since minimum reliability estimates of .50 to .60 are considered sufficient for early stages of research (Nunnally 1967), measures used in this exploratory study can be regarded as relatively reliable. Table 3 reports these alpha values along with mean scores and other measures of the study variables.

Table 1 shows means and standard deviations of all the importance ratings of job characteristics used to measure work motivations. On a scale of 1 to 7 (where 1 = not important and 7 = extremely important), mean ratings show that variables intrinsic in nature (e.g., working for a company with which I am proud to be associated; the job will provide me with feelings of worthwhile accomplishment) were rated more highly than other types (e.g., extrinsic) of variables.

Job characteristics items were subjected to a factor analysis using a varimax rotation. Components with eigenvalues greater than 1.0 were rotated (Tatsuoka 1971). As shown in Table 2, five major factors emerged, with each item assigned to the factor for which it had the highest loading. Factor loadings ranged from a low of .41 for "proud company associations" to .80 for "offers work hours I want." Except for a few moderate loadings, most items loaded quite strongly on their assigned factors. The five resulting factors were named as follows: Factor 1, social recognition and organizational identification; Factor 2, income and career growth; Factor 3, attention and approval; Factor 4, personal fulfillment and job challenge; and Factor 5, autonomy and control. Most of these factors had some similarity to important reasons why people become direct salespeople as found in an earlier Direct Selling Association study (Harris 1977). To some extent, that similarity reflects on the appropriate-

Table 3. Measurements of the Study Variables

Variables	Number of items	Range	Mean	S.D.	Alpha
Independent variables:					
Factor 1	8	8-56	40.7	8.5	.83
Factor 2	6	6-42	35.6	4.8	.77
Factor 3	4	4-28	21.3	4.6	.74
Factor 4	5	5-35	29.6	4.4	.77
Factor 5	3	3-21	16.8	3.1	.50
Dependent variables:					
Commitment	15	15-105	67.3	19.7	.92
Satisfaction	10	10-70	49.1	15.1	.95
Performance	7	7-35	20.2	6.1	.83
Turnover	1	1-6	3.6	2.0	n.a.

Note: Names assigned the Factors are given in a footnote to
       Table 2. Larger values indicate greater importance in the
       case of Factors 1 to 5, greater degrees of organizational
       commitment and job satisfaction, more positive performance
       ratings, and a greater likelihood of quitting.

ness of the factors extracted in this study. These results provide a positive answer to the first research question, indicating that there are different and identifiable work motivations which describe why people become direct selling salespeople.

The second research question is addressed through correlation analysis. Table 4 shows correlation coefficients between work motivation factors and work outcomes. Factor 1 was shown to be significantly related to all the criterion variables. The strongest correlation ($r = .337$) was found between Factor 1 and organizational commitment, suggesting that salespeople who seek a job for

Table 4. Correlations Between Work Motivation Factors and Work Outcomes

Work Motivation Factors	Correlation with:			
	Commitment	Satisfaction	Performance	Turnover
Factor 1: Social recognition and organizational identification	.337**	.320**	.240**	-.261**
Factor 2: Income and career growth	.073	.025	.036	-.005
Factor 3: Attention and approval	.025	.010	.031	.010
Factor 4: Personal fulfill- ment and job challenge	.142**	.137**	.089	-.079
Factor 5: Autonomy and control	.181**	.201**	.088	-.180**

**Significant at p<.01.

reasons of social recognition and organizational identification are likely to demonstrate a higher degree of organizational commitment. The significant correlations between Factor 1 and job satisfaction, performance, and quitting intentions show that such salespeople are not only likely to be more satisfied with their direct sales jobs, but also perform well on the job and are less likely to quit.

Factors 2 and 3 did not show any significant relationships with any of the dependent variables. As a result, it can be concluded that, for salespeople to whom either income and career growth or attention and approval are important, such motivational factors do not affect their commitment, satisfaction, work performance, and quitting intentions.

Factor 4, personal fulfillment and job challenge, showed significant relationships with organizational commitment (r = .142) and job satisfaction (r = .137). Likewise, Factor 5, autonomy and control, demonstrated significant relationships with all criterion variables except job performance. Though these correlations were of small magnitude, they were statistically significant at p < .01. These correlations suggest that variables related to personal fulfillment and challenge as well as to job autonomy and control will positively affect direct salespeople's organizational commitment and job satisfaction. Further, salespeople who place high value on autonomy and control will be less likely to quit.

Based on these results, there is also support for a positive answer to research question 2. Thus, there are associations between some of the work motivations for joining a direct selling sales force and work outcomes, especially organizational commitment and job satisfaction as well as turnover and job performance to a lesser extent. But other work motivations do not relate to these dependent variables, reinforcing the idea in research question 2 that some work motivations are more favorable than others in relating to desirable work outcomes.

DISCUSSION AND IMPLICATIONS

The results of this exploratory study suggest that the reasons people take jobs in direct selling (i.e., their work motivations) may affect their work outcomes, such as organizational commitment, job satisfaction, performance, and propensity to quit. While these associations did not hold for all five work motivations with all four work outcomes, they did occur in nine instances out of the total of twenty studied–far more than would be expected by chance. Based on these findings, some implications for managers as well as researchers emerge.

Managers in direct selling firms should seek employees who will experience desirable work outcomes, both for the employees' sake as well as for company success. Using the results from this study as shown in Table 4, it seems clear that management should direct its recruiting messages to appeal to persons whose work motivations are defined by Factors 1, 4, and 5. Attracting persons who are low in these motivations, or who place higher priority on Factor 2 and 3 motivations, will be less productive in yielding desirable work outcomes. What this suggests, for example, is that recruiting efforts should place less emphasis on substantial earnings opportunities

(Factor 2) and more emphasis on social rewards (Factor 1), personal fulfillment (Factor 4) and autonomy (Factor 5).

Researchers should find these results of interest also since reasons for taking a selling job (i.e., work motivations) have not previously been incorporated in studies of organizational commitment, job satisfaction, or turnover among salespeople. The results here suggest that the addition of work motivations in future studies might improve the results in terms of reducing unexplained variance. Alternatively, work motivations might prove to be useful moderating variables which would show that some types of work motivations engender stronger relationships than do other types of work motivations. For instance, just as performance has been found to be a moderating variable between job satisfaction and turnover (Futrell and Parasuraman 1984), so might work motivations be a moderating variable between organizational commitment or various measures of performance and turnover.

Finally, more research is needed to confirm or sharpen the findings in this study. For instance, different results might be obtained if other job characteristics were used in addition to, or in place of, those in Table 1. The relationships between work motivations and work outcomes should also be tested in other selling contexts, since the results here might be specific to sales jobs for direct selling companies only. Finally, other work outcomes should be examined for their relationships to work motivations as well. Such variables as met expectations, job clarity, effort, and tenure might demonstrate significant relationships with work motivations in a variety of sales settings.

REFERENCES

Behrman, Douglas N. and William D. Perreault, Jr. (1982), "Measuring the Performance of Industrial Salespersons," *Journal of Business Research*, 10 (September), 355-370.

Becherer, Richard C., Fred W. Morgan, and Lawrence M. Richard (1982), "The Job Characteristics of Industrial Salespersons: Relationship to Motivation and Satisfaction," *Journal of Marketing*, 46 (Fall), 125-135.

Biggart, Nicole W. (1989), *Charismatic Capitalism*, Chicago: University of Chicago Press.

Chonko, Lawrence B. (1986), "Organizational Commitment and the Sales Force," *Journal of Personal Selling & Sales Management,* 6 (November), 19-27.

Futrell, Charles M. and A. Parasuraman (1984), "The Relationship of Satisfaction and Performance to Salesforce Turnover," *Journal of Marketing,* 48 (Fall), 33-40.

Hackman, J. Richard and Greg R. Oldham (1974), *The Job Diagnostic Survey: An Instrument for Diagnosing the Motivational Potential of Jobs,* Technical Report No. 4, New Haven, CT: Yale University, Department of Administrative Sciences.

Hackman, J. Richard and Greg R. Oldham (1975), "Development of the Job Diagnostic Survey," *Journal of Applied Psychology,* 60 (April), 159-170.

Harris, Louis, and Associates (1977), "Highlights of a Comprehensive Survey of the Direct Selling Industry," Washington, D.C.: Direct Selling Association.

Ingram, Thomas N., Keun S. Lee, and Steven J. Skinner (1989), "An Empirical Assessment of Salesperson Motivation, Commitment, and Job Outcomes," *Journal of Personal Selling & Sales Management,* 9 (Fall), 25-33.

Johnston, Mark W., P. Rajan Varadarajan, Charles M. Futrell, and Jeffrey Sager (1987), "The Relationship Between Organizational Commitment, Job Satisfaction, and Turnover Among New Salespeople," *Journal of Personal Selling & Sales Management,* 7 (November), 29-38.

Mabe, Paul A., III, and Stephen G. West (1982), "Validity of Self-Evaluation of Ability: A Review and Meta-Analysis," *Journal of Applied Psychology,* 67 (June), 280-296.

Nunnally, Jum C. (1967), *Psychometric Theory,* New York: McGraw-Hill Book Company.

Porter, Lyman W., R. M. Steers, R. T. Mowday, and P. V. Boulian (1974), "Organizational Commitment, Job Satisfaction, and Turnover Among Psychiatric Technicians," *Journal of Applied Psychology,* 59 (October), 603-609.

Sager, Jeffrey K. and Mark W. Johnston (1989), "Antecedents and Outcomes of Organizational Commitment: A Study of Salespeople," *Journal of Personal Selling & Sales Management,* 9 (Spring), 30-41.

Still, Lonnie V. (1983), "Part-Time Versus Full-Time Salespeople: Individual Attributes, Organizational Commitment, and Work Attitudes," *Journal of Retailing,* 59 (Summer), 55-79.

Tatsuoka, Maurice A. (1971), *Multivariate Analysis,* New York: John Wiley & Sons, Inc.

Thistlethwaite, Paul et al. (1985), *Direct Selling in MidAmerica,* Macomb, IL: Center for Business and Economic Research, Western Illinois University.

Tyagi, Pradeep K. (1985), "Work Motivation Through the Design of Salesperson Jobs," *Journal of Personal Selling & Sales Management,* 5 (May), 41-51.

Wotruba, Thomas R. (1989), "The Effect of Goal-Setting on the Performance of Independent Sales Agents in Direct Selling," *Journal of Personal Selling & Sales Management,* 9 (Spring), 22-29.

Wotruba, Thomas R. (1990a), "The Relationship of Job Image, Performance, and

Job Satisfaction to Inactivity-Proneness of Direct Salespeople," *Journal of the Academy of Marketing Science,* 18 (Spring), 113-121.

Wotruba, Thomas R. (1990b), "Full-time versus Part-time Salespeople: A Comparison on Job Satisfaction, Performance, and Turnover in Direct Selling," *International Journal of Research in Marketing,* 7 (December), 97-108.

Wotruba, Thomas R. (1992), "Direct Selling in the Year 2000," in *The Future of U.S. Retailing,* Robert A. Peterson, ed., New York: Quorum Books, 187-211.

Wotruba, Thomas R., Donald Sciglimpaglia, and Pradeep K. Tyagi (1987), "Toward a Model of Turnover in Direct Selling Organizations," in *Marketing Theory,* AMA Winter Educators' Conference Proceedings, Russell W. Belk and Gerald Zaltman, eds., Chicago: American Marketing Association, 348-353.

Wotruba, Thomas R. and Pradeep K. Tyagi (1991), "Met Expectations and Turnover in Direct Selling," *Journal of Marketing,* 55 (July), 24-35.

The Role of Personal Selling
in Direct Sales Organizations

Thomas N. Ingram

SUMMARY. This article reviews several developments in the operating environment of direct sales organizations which affect the strategic roles of the personal selling function. The most likely strategic
roles are discussed, and tactical implications for direct salespeople
and sales managers are suggested. To fully realize the multiple benefits of personal selling, direct sales organizations must be firmly
committed to the trust-based relationship selling paradigm. Such a
sales approach requires salespeople to move past a short-term transaction orientation to fulfill roles such as counselors, ombudsmen,
and ambassadors.

For direct sales organizations, defining the role of personal selling is somewhat like defining the role of athletes for a successful
sports team. It is a given that the athletes (or direct salespeople) will
indeed play a critical role in the success or failure of their organizations. In both cases, the task of role definition centers on strategy
and tactics. It is also true that these key players will require a
tremendous amount of support to survive, much less flourish, in an
increasingly competitive environment.

The purpose of this article is to define the role of personal selling
in direct sales organizations. More precisely, an attempt will be
made to synthesize several important developments in the marketing environment which have strategic relevance to direct sales organizations. Several strategic roles for the sales function will then be
presented, followed by a discussion of tactical implications for the

Thomas N. Ingram is Professor of Marketing and Holder of the Sales and
Marketing Executives Chair in Sales Excellence at Memphis State University.

personal selling function. The framework for the article is shown in Figure 1.

Readers should be advised that very little research has been conducted, or at least made public, on the role of direct salespeople within their organizations. The limited research on direct selling has concentrated primarily on sales management issues such as job satisfaction, turnover, and performance (Wotruba 1990; Wotruba and Tyagi 1991). Since prior research on the role of personal selling in direct sales organizations is practically non-existent, this article attempts to integrate thoughts from marketing management, channels, and personal selling in general to gain insights and encourage future discussion and research.

MARKETING DEVELOPMENTS

As suggested in Figure 1, there are six especially noteworthy developments in marketing that will strongly influence the role of personal selling in direct sales organizations in the next decade: the fragmentation of markets; the globalization of markets; the necessity for a multiple channels approach; the increasing importance of market timing considerations; the emergence of speed as a major competitive weapon; and the emergence of trust-based relationship selling as the major paradigm for personal selling. These developments are not unique to the task environment of direct sales organizations, but this in no way diminishes their importance as influencers of personal selling strategy and tactics. Indeed, these factors call for major redefinitions of the role of personal selling in many direct sales organizations.

Market Fragmentation

The past three decades have seen the emergence, growth, and now decline of a so-called mass market that could be reached and moved to action via standardized selling strategies. In the current environment, successful companies key more on selective market coverage, and concentrate on developing selling methods more suited to local conditions. This is not to suggest that standardized methods are completely antiquated, only that increasingly fragmented markets often require tailored approaches.

Figure 1
Framework for Defining the Role of
Personal Selling in Direct Sales
Organizations

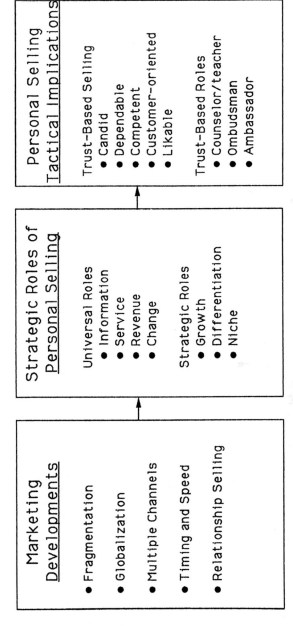

Marketing
Developments

● Fragmentation

● Globalization

● Multiple Channels

● Timing and Speed

● Relationship Selling

Strategic Roles of
Personal Selling

Universal Roles
● Information
● Service
● Revenue
● Change

Strategic Roles
● Growth
● Differentiation
● Niche

Personal Selling
Tactical Implications

Trust-Based Selling
● Candid
● Dependable
● Competent
● Customer-oriented
● Likable

Trust-Based Roles
● Counselor/teacher
● Ombudsman
● Ambassador

Market fragmentation, or the splintering of previously defined market segments into sub-segments, forces direct sales organizations to think about two basic options. First is the notion of market "ownership through leadership" (Mckenna 1991). This perspective is based on the notion that the true goal of marketing is not merely to create products of sufficient value to allow a profitable operation of the firm. Rather, the ownership-through-leadership philosophy dictates a single-minded focus on one part of the market, ultimately resulting in the erection of a significant buffer from competitive forces. For example, London-based Alfred Dunhill focuses on meeting the professional clothing needs of executives, and may approximate "ownership" of the at-work-site-tailoring aspect of this market (Ballen 1988).

At the other extreme of how to approach fragmenting markets is the concept of expeditionary marketing. This concept calls for companies to "escape the tyranny of served markets" (Hazel and Prahalad 1991). This perspective is not overly concerned about the ratio of successful market ventures to the number of ventures attempted. Rather, expeditionary marketing concentrates more on the total number of successes achieved. While expeditionary marketing sounds riskier than ownership-through-leadership, it may be the wiser direction if the unserved potential market is more promising than the currently-served market.

It should be noted that the expeditionary marketing perspective is broad enough to encompass the ownership-through-leadership philosophy. In true expeditionary fashion, companies would be expected to lead–not follow–their customers in terms of new product ideas and the implementation of new ways for consumers to buy. For example, direct sales organizations, such as Mary Kay Cosmetics, have practiced expeditionary marketing in the implementation of direct mail ordering alternatives for consumers.

Globalization

The globalization of markets is perhaps the most significant development in the marketing environment of direct sales organizations. The strong demand for Westernized products in newly-opened European and Asian markets has spurred growth for many direct sales organizations, including Avon, Time Life Books, Amway, Tupperware, and Mary Kay Cosmetics.

The personal selling dimension is particularly appropriate for the development of non-domestic markets when compared to other elements of the promotional mix. Time Life Books, based in the United States, has chosen to use personal selling in Asia, in spite of its exclusive (and highly successful) use of direct-response mail and advertising used in all its other markets. Translation problems are lessened, cultural differences are dissipated, set-up time is minimal, and sunk channel costs are low. Further, the high level of salesperson motivation in many countries new to free enterprise is cited as an advantage of personal selling by direct sales organizations.

Multiple Channel Approaches

Market fragmentation and globalization are among the driving forces which have fueled a trend toward multiple-channel approaches for a large variety of goods and services. Another contributing factor is that it is simply good business to make it easy for shoppers to buy where they want to, from the outlet of their choice. Marketing giants like Goodyear and IBM have recently intensified their efforts to reach consumers through new channels, as have many of the leading direct sales organizations.

Since the roles of direct salespeople can be redefined to productively coexist with other channels, the trend toward the establishment of multiple channels should bode well for personal selling as a strategic alternative. For example, Mary Kay Cosmetics has realized substantial benefits from tying its direct mail and telephone ordering system to the salesforce. As a result, the company stands well-positioned to compete for cosmetics customers in the coming decade, as struggling department stores are likely to be short on promotion support, in-store selling effort, and personalized service (Hoke 1989; Zellner 1991).

Timing and Speed as Competitive Variables

More than ever, timing and speed will determine success in the marketplace (Stalk and Hout 1990). This favors direct sales organizations in general, and their personal selling operations in particular. As the Eastern European markets became unexpectedly available in the early 1990s, direct sales organizations were among the first to make significant inroads. The pent-up demand for consumer goods in these countries represented a tremendous opportunity for manufacturers, but only to those that could quickly implement a low-cost distribution system.

Direct selling organizations have also done well in the booming Asian market, where GNP will exceed that of North America and Europe combined by the year 2000. Take, for example, the case of Avon, which entered the Asian cosmetics market in 1985. Within four years, Avon's sales in Asia rose to $400 million, and the figure has been rapidly growing. Avon next moved into China in the early 1990s, and future plans call for an expansion to two million salespeople in China within a decade (Nelson 1991).

Trust-Based Relationship Selling

Direct selling organizations can benefit from the consumer-preference-driven trend toward selling via trust-based relationships. This is true only to the extent that sales organizations take responsibility for what transpires during consumer/salesperson interactions. As has been proven in the automobile industry, consumers will severely punish an industry that is willing to allow unprofessional sales tactics to dominate. Consumers have sent a clear message to automobile manufacturers which indicates that they are tired of the tricks and gimmicks typically used to sell cars (Woodruff 1992). Further, evidence suggests that automobile buyers will respond favorably to straightforward sales appeals (Swan and Oliver 1991).

This lesson should not be lost on direct sales organizations, even though the task of regulating independent salespeople and their sales messages can be difficult. If the basic thesis is correct–that earning the customer's trust will be of paramount importance for sales success–then an appropriate investment in training and field guidance must be made. For example, Fuller Brush has established its own FBI–Fuller Brush Inspectors–to monitor its distributors in an attempt to maintain integrity and build trust with its customers (Gabriel 1992).

STRATEGIC ROLE OF PERSONAL SELLING

Personal selling is capable of fulfilling multiple roles depending on the corporate, business unit, and marketing objectives of the firm. To some extent, however, personal selling assumes four universal roles in all direct sales organizations. These universal roles are related to salepeoples' involvement in information flows, customer service activities, revenue generation, and the processes of change, including the diffusion of innovation. The fulfillment of these universal roles is essential for the success of any direct sales organization, and personal selling generally contributes more to fulfillment of these roles than any other functional area.

Adding Value with Information

As business proceeds in the much-ballyhooed knowledge-explosion era, those in possession of valuable information are extremely important to the success of any organization. Salespeople add utility to the products and services they sell by passing on worthwhile information to the consumer. They also add value to the sales organization's research and consumer feedback efforts. The importance of maintaining close contact with customers has been learned the hard way by more than one direct sales organization. For example, Avon's president of the U.S. direct selling division, in reviewing the company's struggles in the late 1980s, says Avon "wasn't in touch with the customer" (Markovits 1988).

Customer Service Activities

The lines between customer service and personal selling will continue to blur. This represents a significant opportunity for direct sales organizations, as the sales process has necessarily become service-oriented–not simply after the sale, but also before and during sales presentations.

Revenue Generation

With a lot of support from other functional areas, personal selling is the primary generator of revenue. This revenue comes directly from sales transactions, and, in many cases, through salespeople's recruiting efforts over a longer time horizon. The task of recruiting effective salespeople will remain a challenge, especially in well-developed economies, and this future-oriented function needs considerable upgrading in most direct sales organizations.

Change Processes

Personal selling offers direct sales organizations something desperately needed in a dynamic environment–legions of change agents. Salespeople will continue to work alone and with advertising to tap new markets and introduce new products. The personal selling function is virtually indispensable in facilitating change in the marketplace, and can be especially influential when the total salesforce numbers in the hundreds of thousands as it does with many leading direct sellers.

STRATEGIC ROLES FOR PERSONAL SELLING

Personal selling strategies depend on overall corporate strategy and, if present, the strategy for individual business units. It is expected that direct sales organizations will continue to seek market share and overall sales volume growth as basic objectives. There is little evidence to suggest that direct sales organizations will pursue alternatives such as harvesting, divestiture, or liquidation as basic objectives in the coming decade. Some direct companies will, however, divest non-direct-sales holdings in order to concentrate on the growth objectives of direct selling units. For example, Avon has divested its health care and retirement home operations, perhaps because direct selling offers a more attractive way to build profitable volume (Hager 1991).

Corporate Growth Orientation and Personal Selling

There are three basic orientations toward corporate growth: intensive growth, diversification growth, and acquisition (Ingram and

LaForge 1992). Most direct sales organizations will follow the intensive growth direction, which focuses on the development of existing business. New products will be introduced, but most will not be radical departures from existing product lines.

The sales function is extremely active when intensive growth is sought through internal development. The amount of selling effort should be intensified for existing products. Training should be a priority, with a focus on improving sales productivity. Motivational programs must remain a strong part of the support system in order to effectively introduce new products and help to moderate salesforce turnover.

Direct sales organizations should not assume that increasing sales effort will lead to improved sales results. Limited research indicates, for example, that goal-setting for relatively new (less than a year in direct sales) salespeople led to higher levels of effort, but not performance (Wotruba 1989). Care must be taken to not only increase selling effort, but to ensure that efforts are properly directed and supported via training, supervision, and motivation.

Generic Strategy and Personal Selling

Porter (1980) presents three generic strategies which could be used to pursue corporate growth objectives (Porter 1980). These are low-cost supplier, differentiation, and niche strategies. Direct sales organizations are unlikely to pursue low-cost supplier strategies, which translate into selling on the basis of a low price. Rather, they will continue to follow differentiation and niche strategies.

Differentiation requires that a company develop a perceived uniqueness which will somewhat reduce the effectiveness of competitors' efforts. In direct selling, this means that the salesforce must be able to sell non-price benefits and be extremely responsive to customer needs. When coupled with ambitious growth objectives, a differentiation strategy may require extensive prospecting by the salesforce. In brief, this strategy requires a well-rounded, high-quality salesforce (Cron and Levy 1987).

Niche strategies will be followed by some direct selling firms. Niche involves the selection of a particular target market, and then attempting to dominate this part of the market by meeting specialized customer needs. Absolute market share is not important, but rather the focus is on high-margin volume. The previously-mentioned Dunhill firm uses a niche strategy to meet the convenience and high-quality clothing needs of executives by sending their salespeople/tailors directly to the executives' offices for fittings (Batten 1988).

The role of salespeople in implementing niche strategies is to provide expert opinion to customers to warrant the relatively high prices being charged. Training must be taken seriously, and recruiting becomes more oriented toward quality rather than quantity of new salespeople. In terms of the fundamental sales message, niche strategies, like differentiation strategies, should focus on non-price benefits.

Most existing direct selling organizations will diligently try to continue to serve existing markets while also seeking growth through globalization or expansion of their current customer bases. In this regard, these firms are what Miles and Snow (1978) would call "analyzer" firms (Miles and Snow 1978). Salespeople in such firms must really be versatile, and fulfill all of the universal roles of salespeople. To generate revenue, they must provide valuable information to customers and to the selling firm, be active in service roles, and act as change agents in the introduction of new products and promotional programs.

PERSONAL SELLING TACTICAL IMPLICATIONS

The sales tactics necessary to carry out niche and differentiation strategies can be summarized within a trust-building framework. This will require that direct salespeople look beyond short-term volume as their primary goal.

Trust-Based Selling

To achieve trust-based relationships with customers, salespeople must be candid, dependable, competent, customer-oriented, and likable (Hawes et al. 1989). Specific tactical suggestions for each of these dimensions are given in Figure 2.

Figure 2

Suggestions for Trust-Based Relationship Selling

Candor: (Words)
- Presentations are balanced and fair (e.g., product limitations as well as advantages are discussed).
- What is said agrees with what the buyer knows to be true.
- Support evidence and demonstrations are credible.
- Subsequent events prove statements to be true.

Dependability: (Actions)
- Actions fulfill prior verbal promises.
- Action fits a pattern of prior dependable actions.
- Promises can realistically be met.

Competence: (Ability)
- Technical command of products and applications.
- Statepeople have the skill, knowledge, time and resources to do what the buyer wants.
- Words and actions are consistent with a professional "image."

Customer-Orientation: (Intent)
- Buyer's needs are clarified and treated with respect.
- Clear statements of benefits.
- Advise rather than "sell." (Don't push a product the buyer doesn't need).

Likability: (Personality)
- Make efficient use of the buyer's time.
- Be courteous and polite.

Source: Adapted from Doyle, Stephen X. and George Thomas Roth (1992). "The Use of Insight Coaching to Improve Relationship Selling", *Journal of Personal Selling and Sales Management*, 12 (Winter), 62.

As suggested in Figure 2, sales presentations are becoming a no-nonsense affair. Successful presentations will increasingly be those that are devoid of gimmicks, and artificial formulas for executing the presentation. For example, the highly structured Attention-Interest-Desire-Action (AIDA) paradigm for making the sale is slowly but surely becoming obsolete (Ingram 1990). Never truly customer-oriented, the AIDA approach is being replaced by sales presentations which require careful listening, questioning, and flexibility on the part of the salesperson.

Trust-Based Sales Roles

The initial generation of profitable revenue is only one of the benefits of trust-based selling for a direct salesforce. The most significant benefits to the selling firm are a potential lifetime revenue stream and the referral of prospects from the satisfied customer base.

In practicing trust-based selling, direct sellers would be implementing what Kotler calls "wrap-around marketing" (Caruso 1992). This means that customers must be pre-sold, sold, and then, in effect, post-sold. To identify direct selling tactics that are likely to be more important in wrap-around marketing, three tactical roles come to mind. These roles are: counselor/teacher; ombudsman; and ambassador (Magrath and Hardy 1987).

The counselor/teacher role requires that salespeople must be experts in terms of understanding customer needs and how their products can meet those needs. They must also be excellent listeners, and highly-effective presenters.

The ombudsman role requires the salesperson to be a customer-oriented problem solver who can take decisive action when customer satisfaction is threatened. As much as direct sales organizations would like for every order to be entered, shipped, and billed correctly, mistakes will occur. Consumers are aware that perfection is probably an unrealistic expectation, but they do expect near-perfection–and they definitely expect salespeople to quickly respond to problems. In this role, salespeople will be able to rely on more timely information, and hopefully more accurate information, through data-based technology advances now being put into place in many direct selling organizations.

The ambassador role will be especially important as new products are introduced, and as recruiting adopts a more professional approach in the coming years. A large portion of any direct seller's credibility is attributable to its salespeople, and the ambassador role allows salespeople to contribute to the overall image of the organization in a meaningful way.

CONCLUSION

Direct selling organizations are well-positioned to capitalize on fast-developing, fragmenting markets, and to realize the benefits of globalization. These firms are also well-suited to blend multiple sales channels, with the possibility that personal selling could adopt different roles over time to match market opportunities. By focusing more on generating revenue through long-term trust-based relationships with customers, direct sellers can strengthen their market positions. This will require that direct salespeople act more as counselors/teachers, ombudsmen, and ambassadors to satisfy customer needs. Essentially, this will call for a strong emphasis on professionalism and making full use of sales technology to maintain close contact with prospects and customers before, during, and after the sale.

REFERENCES

Ballen, Kate (1988). Get ready for shopping at work. *Fortune*, 117 (February 15), 97-98.

Caruso, Thomas E. (1992). Kotler: future marketers will focus on customer data base to compete globally. *Marketing News*, June 8, 21.

Cron, William L. and Michael Levy (1987). Sales management performance evaluation: a residual income perspective. *Journal of Personal Selling and Sales Management*, 7 (August), 57-66.

Hazel, Gary, and C.K. Prahalad (1991). Corporate imagination and expeditionary marketing. *Harvard Business Review*, 69 (July-August), 81-92.

Gabriel, Gail (1992). Reborn after 85 years. *Success* (April), 16.

Hager, Bruce (1991). Despite the facelift, Avon is sagging. *Business Week*, December 2, 101-102.

Hawes, Jon. M., Kenneth E. Mast, and John E. Swan (1989). Trust earning perceptions of sellers and buyers. *Journal of Personal Selling and Sales Management*, 9 (Spring), 59-67.

Hoke, Pete (1989). Glamorous database. *Direct Marketing* (July), 54-68; and Zellner, Wendy (1991), *Business Week*, December 2, 1991, 102.

Ingram, Thomas N. (1990). Improving salesforce productivity: a critical review of the personal selling process. *Review of Business*, 12 (Summer), 7-12+.

Ingram, Thomas N. and Raymond W. LaForge (1992). *Sales management: analysis and decision making.* Fort Worth, The Dryden Press.

Magrath, Allan J. and Kenneth C. Hardy (1987). Factory salesmen's roles with industrial distributors. *Industrial Marketing Management,* 16, 160-169.

Markovits, Paul (1988). Direct selling is alive and well. *Sales and Marketing Management,* (August), 76-78.

Mckenna, Regis (1991). Marketing is everything. *Harvard Business Review,* 69 (January-February), 65-79.

Miles, Raymond E. and Charles C. Snow (1978). *Organizational strategy, structure, and process.* New York, McGraw-Hill, Inc.

Nelson, Kelly (1991), Door-to-door in Guangzhou. *The China Business Review,* (March-April), 40-41.

Porter, Michael E. (1980). *Competitive strategy: techniques for analyzing industries and competition.* New York, The Free Press.

Stalk, George Jr. and Thomas M. Hout (1990). *Competing against time.* New York, The Free Press.

Swan, John E. and Richard E. Oliver (1991). An applied analysis of buyer equity perceptions and satisfaction with automobile salespeople. *Journal of Personal Selling and Sales Management,* 11 (Spring), 16-26.

Woodruff, David (1992). What's this—car dealers with souls? *Business Week,* April 6, 1992, 66-67.

Wotruba, Thomas R. (1989). The effect of goal-setting on the performance of independent sales agents in direct selling. *Journal of Personal Selling and Sales Management,* 9 (Spring), 22-29.

Sex-Role Self-Concept
and Direct Sales Success
in Minority Saleswomen

Harold B. Teer
Jerome J. Tobacyk
Lyndon E. Dawson, Jr.

SUMMARY. Relationships between sex-role self-concept and sales performance were investigated in a sample of majority Black female direct saleswomen. Although neither Masculinity, Femininity, nor Androgyny were associated with higher sales performance, data revealed strong evidence for selection factors in these saleswomen. Sixty-four percent of these salespersons recorded an Androgynous sex-role self-concept, compared to 29% expected from norms. Further, 75% of the saleswomen recorded high levels of Masculinity, compared to 45% expected from norms.

During the past thirty years American society has experienced massive changes in normative expectations of gender-appropriate behaviors of men and women. Because women comprise about 80% of the sales force in the direct selling industry (Direct Selling Association, 1982), knowledge of sex-role self-concept of women may be particularly important for the direct sales industry. This paper reports an investigation of relationships between the sex-role self-concept of a group of minority direct saleswomen and their sales performance.

Hal B. Teer is Associate Professor of Marketing and Director of the Center for Retailing at James Madison University. Jerome J. Tobacyk is Professor of Psychology at Louisiana Tech University. Lyndon E. Dawson, Jr. is Professor of Marketing at Louisiana Tech University.

Bem (1974) presented an innovative theoretical formulation of sex-role self-concept, and constructed an assessment instrument (Bem Sex Role Inventory; BSRI) with fidelity to her theoretical formulation. Briefly, Bem proposed a dualistic model of sex-role self-concept based on the notion that masculinity and femininity are separate, independent constructs, each present in different degrees within each person. According to this dualistic model, a person may concurrently possess varying levels of *both* masculinity and femininity.

This dualistic model differs sharply from the traditional bipolar model of sex-role self-concept, in which masculinity and femininity are assumed to lie on a single, unidimensional continuum. According to Bem's dualistic formulation, psychologically androgynous persons (i.e., those concurrently possessing high levels of both masculinity and femininity) may have an adaptive advantage over masculine males and feminine females. This proposed adaptive advantage of androgynous persons is linked to their presumably greater behavioral flexibility. That is, androgynous persons may enact either masculine or feminine behaviors, as required by the situation. In contrast, the behavior of strongly sex-typed persons is presumably constrained by relatively inflexible sex-role stereotypic behavioral repertoires.

This argument for the adaptive advantages of psychological androgyny appears theoretically reasonable. However, the empirical evidence is mixed. In both the psychological and consumer behavior domains, psychological androgyny and masculinity have each demonstrated positive relationships with measures of effective functioning–particularly as compared to femininity (see Cook, 1985, pp. 99-100; Stern, 1988, for reviews). However, there is emerging consensus that the adaptive advantages associated with psychological androgyny are simply due to the high level of masculinity characterizing androgynous persons, rather than due to their concurrently high levels of both masculinity and femininity (Adams & Sherer, 1982; Antill & Cunningham, 1979; Barak & Stern, 1986; Lee & Scheuer, 1982).

A review of the literature reveals that many stereotypically masculine dispositions are positively associated with various indicators of sales performance. These stereotypically masculine dispositional correlates of sales performance include gender (Swan & Futrell, 1978), physical stature (Lamont & Lundstrom, 1977), aggressiveness (Oda, 1982; 1983), determination (Tibbitts, 1976), dominance (Deb, 1983), ego drive (Lamont & Lundstrom, 1977), independence/self-reliance (Hartman, 1973; Oda, 1983), leadership (Oda, 1983), motivation (Ghiselli, 1969), openness (Barrick & Mount, 1991), and self-confidence (Oda, 1983; Tibbitts, 1976).

However, theoretically, it seems reasonable that psychological androgyny may be even more strongly associated with sales success than masculinity. This is because, in addition to possessing those stereotypically masculine traits associated with sales success, the presumably greater behavioral flexibility of androgynous saleswomen might allow them to modify their interpersonal behaviors to fit the needs of different clients in different situations. More specifically, androgynous saleswomen might be more able to engage in adaptive selling behaviors (Spiro & Weitz, 1990) than their masculine or feminine sex-typed counterparts.

This paper investigates relationships between the sex-role self-concept of minority direct saleswomen and their direct sales performance. Three formulations of the implications of sex-role self-concept for direct sales performance are compared: (1) the traditional formulation that the sex-role conventionally appropriate to one's gender is associated with higher sales performance, (2) the formulation that psychological androgyny (i.e., concurrently high levels of both masculinity and femininity) is associated with higher sales performance, and (3) the formulation that level of masculinity alone is associated with higher sales performance.

METHOD

A systematic random sampling procedure was used to select 500 saleswomen from a population of 1,815 female direct saleswomen associated with a national direct sales company which sold one line of consumer products–perfumes–through direct selling methods. A two stage data collection procedure was used: (1) an informational letter, signed by the company's president and requesting participation in the forthcoming study, was sent to all 500 women in the sampling frame; and (2) four days later a letter containing the Bem Sex Role Inventory (BSRI) and a post-paid return envelope was sent to each potential respondent. Of the 500 saleswomen in the test group, 153 returned usable questionnaires. Based on a uniform formulation for measuring response rates for survey research by the Council of American Survey Research Organizations (1982), the response rate was 35%. Information on sales performance (i.e., total sales in dollar amount for the period January to April, 1985) was provided by the company. The racial makeup of the sample was about 70% Black, 5% Hispanic, and 25% Caucasian.

METHOD OF ANALYSIS

Sex-role self-concept was assessed by the standard procedure of using median scores for females from Bem's (1981) normative sample as criteria. Each respondent was classified as follows, depending on whether her masculinity and femininity scale scores were above or below the median of the normative sample: (1) Undifferentiated–below the median for both masculinity and femininity; (2) Masculine–above the median for masculinity and below the median for femininity; (3) Feminine–above the median for femininity and below the median for masculinity; and (4) Androgynous–above the median for both masculinity and femininity. Group sizes were: Undifferentiated, $n = 9$; Masculine, $n = 17$; Feminine, $n = 31$; Androgynous, $n = 96$.

Two procedures were used to test hypotheses. First, a Oneway Analysis of Variance (ANOVA) was conducted with group membership as a four-level predictor variable (Undifferentiated, Masculine, Feminine, Androgynous) and with total product sales for January-April, 1985 as the outcome variable. A significant overall F statistic would be followed by post hoc tests to determine which specific group differences are significant, which, in turn, would reveal which formulations are supported. Second, two Pearson product-moment correlations were computed–one between masculinity scores and the outcome variable, the other between femininity scores and the outcome variable.

RESULTS AND DISCUSSION

The F statistic for the Oneway ANOVA was not statistically significant (F 3, 149 = 1.87, p > .05). Thus, there were no significant group mean differences in total sales for the test period. The group means for the outcome variable were: Masculine, M = \$486, SD = \$1042; Undifferentiated, M = \$411, SD = \$453; Androgynous, M = \$245, SD = \$452; Feminine, M = \$138, SD = \$222. The results of the Pearson correlations corroborate these findings. The correlations between both masculinity scores and femininity scores with the outcome variable were not significant (respectively, r's = .12 & −.04, ns).

These findings indicate no significant relationship between sex-role self-concept and total sales for the test period. None of the three formulations concerning sex-role self-concept and direct sales success received support. However, the three formulations may not have been adequately tested because of the possibility of selection factors resulting in a restriction in range on the outcome variable scores. It is possible that this sample was largely comprised of saleswomen who were relatively successful at direct selling. Many of the less successful saleswomen may be subject to attrition before working a full six months and therefore, would not be included in this sample.

Additional analyses suggested the presence of sex-role self-concept selection factors in this sample of saleswomen. In this sample, the percentages of saleswomen in each of the four sex-role groups were: Androgynous, 64%; Masculine, 11%; Feminine, 20%; and Undifferentiated, 5%. In contrast, in Bem's (1981) normative sample of women, the corresponding percentages were: Androgynous, 29%; Masculine, 16%; Feminine, 34%; and Undifferentiated, 20%. Thus, there are more than double the percentage of Androgynous women in this sample of saleswomen than in the norming group. A z test for the significance of the difference between two proportions showed that the percentage of Androgynous women in the sample (64%) was significantly greater than the corresponding percentage in the norming group (29%) z = 7.04, p < .001.

Alternatively, if scores above the median on the Masculinity Scale are used as a criterion, 75% of the saleswomen sample are characterized as high (i.e., above the median of the norming group) in masculinity–in contrast to 45% in the norming group. These findings suggest that there may be a selection factor operating in this sample of direct saleswomen. Perhaps in this direct selling company, attitudes, values, and behaviors that characterize Androgynous or Masculine sex-role self-concepts are relatively congruent with the corporate culture and work environment, resulting in retention and subsequent "overrepresentation" of such women. However, this speculation must await further empirical verification because of the dearth of norms for Black females on the Bem Sex Role Inventory. In lieu of the "overrepresentation hypothesis," it is possible that the Androgynous sex-role orientation is simply more frequent in Black females than in the norming groups for the Bem Sex Role Inventory. Thus, although the overrepresentation hypothesis remains plausible, it requires further empirical verification.

The success of direct sales organizations depends importantly on recruiting and retaining individuals within a marketing channel who perform well in sales positions. Deciding who to hire requires the firm to be knowledgeable as to the characteristics of persons who will be successful in direct selling and who will stay with the firm in a sales position. The direct-cost savings achieved in selecting the right person for the direct salesforce can be substantial. Thus, building a successful direct selling marketing channel calls for continuous monitoring of information that links sales performance and personal characteristics.

One such characteristic may be the person's sex-role self-concept. It may be that, generally, direct selling attracts women with androgynous and masculine sex-role self-concepts. This research hypothesized that androgynous females may outperform others because of their presumably greater behavioral flexibility across selling situations.

Because this research frame consisted of a majority Black female direct sales force, additional testing of this hypothesis among a broader range of direct-selling occupations and ethnic groups is needed to develop a final conclusion. However, we also recommend testing the related hypothesis which asserts that, whether or not androgynous persons outperform others in direct sales occupations, they are much more likely than persons with other sex-role self-concepts to enter and remain in the direct sales field.

REFERENCES

Adams, C., & Sherer, M. (1982) Sex-role orientation and psychological adjustment: Comparison of MMPI profiles among college women and housewives. *Journal of Personality Assessment, 46,* 607-613.

Antill, J., & Cunningham, J. (1979) Self esteem as a function of masculinity in both sexes. *Journal of Consulting and Clinical Psychology, 47,* 783-785.

Barrick, M., & Mount, M. (1991) The big five personality dimensions and job performance: A meta-analysis. *Personnel Psychology, 44,* 1-26.

Barak, B., & Stern, B. (1986) Sex-linked trait indexes among baby-boomers and pre-boomers: A research note. In R. Lutz (Ed.), *Advances in Consumer Research, 14,* (pp. 204-209). Ann Arbor, MI: Association for Consumer Research.

Bem, S. (1974) The measurement of psychological androgyny. *Journal of Consulting and Clinical Psychology, 42,* 155-162.

Bem, S. (1981) *Bem sex role inventory: Professional manual.* Palo Alto, CA: Consulting Psychologists Press.

Cook, E. (1985) *Psychological androgyny.* New York: Pergamon Press Inc.

Council of American Survey Research Organizations. (1982) *On the definition of response rates.* Special report, Port Jefferson, NY.

Deb, M. (1983) Sales effectiveness and personality characteristics. *Psychological Research Journal. 7,* 59-67.

Direct Selling Association. (1982) *Backgrounder.* Washington, DC: Direct Selling Association.

Ghiselli, E. (1969) Prediction of success of stockbrokers. *Personnel psychology,* 125-130.

Hartman, T. (1973) Start right by hiring right. *Sales Management, 110,* 70-80.

Lamont, L., & Lundstrom, W. (1977) Identifying successful industrial salesmen by personality and personal characteristics. *Journal of Marketing Research, 14,* 517-529.

Lee, A., & Scheurer, V. (1983) psychological androgyny and aspects of self-image in women and men. *Sex Roles, 9,* 289-306.

Oda, M. (1982) An analysis of relations between personality traits and job performance in sales occupations. *Japanese Journal of Psychology, 53,* 274-280.

Oda, M. (1983) Predicting sales performance of car salesmen by personality traits. *Japanese Journal of Psychology, 54,* 73-80.

Spiro, R., & Weitz, B. (1990) Adaptive selling: Conceptualization, measurement, and nomological validity. *Journal of Marketing Research, 27,* 61-69.

Stern, B. (1988) Sex-role self-concept measures and marketing: A research note. *Psychology and Marketing, 5,* 85-99.

Swan, J., & Futrell, C. (1978) Men versus women in industrial sales: A performance gap. *Industrial Marketing Management, 6,* 369-373.

Tibbitts, F. (1976) What it takes to make it in selling. *Selling and Marketing Management, 117,* 79-80.

Direct Selling:
A Multinational Strategy

Martin L. Schwartz

SUMMARY. This paper provides a method of identifying international markets for which new products marketed via direct selling may be commercially successful. Results of the study indicate that consumer wealth, urbanization and literacy may be used as lead indicators of new product, direct selling success. It is recommended that multinational firms consider the use of a direct selling strategy when launching products into developing markets, and the use of an in-store strategy when launching products into mature markets.

Because global marketing is becoming an increasingly important source of company profits, companies are seeking ways to improve their global competitiveness. Distribution system strategy improvements offer one avenue to achieving a competitive advantage. Recent literature strongly suggests the use of data base oriented, direct marketing as one method of using distribution to achieve this advantage (e.g., Rapp & Collins, 1990; Linen, 1991; Rapp, 1989; Pickholz, 1988; Sanghavi, 1988; Wunderman, 1986). Overlooked in the literature, however, is the use of direct selling as method of creating viable international distribution systems.

Direct selling provides a closer sales-person to customer relationship than is found in direct marketing. (In this paper, direct selling is defined as direct-to-consumer marketing by an in-person sales force. Party plans and door-to-door distribution systems are included.)

Martin L. Schwartz is Associate Professor of Marketing at Miami University, Oxford, OH.

Thanks are given to the Direct Selling Association, Avon Products, Inc., and Professor Kevin McNeilly for the support provided in preparing this paper.

This paper evaluates the use of direct selling as a marketing distribution strategy decision. It is not intended to provide a comprehensive analysis of the entire distribution system, nor of all of the factors which explain commercial success. The question which this paper attempts to answer is, "To what extent do the socioeconomic characteristics of a nation determine whether direct selling is likely to be a viable alternative to in-store sales?"

The model used is:

Success
of
Direct = f(National Socioeconomic Characteristics)
Selling
Launch

This study provides a method of identifying international markets for which new products launched via direct selling may be more successful than are those launched via in-store sales.

BACKGROUND

The theoretical justification for using national socioeconomic characteristics to measure market potential comes from a number of sources. First, direct selling industry personnel have observed a relationship between the two. Avon Products management, for instance, observed that the direct selling of cosmetics and fragrances was more successful in developing countries than in mature ones (O'Halloran et al., 1985). Other direct selling firms observed the same for a variety of products, including cleaning products, kitchen products, jewelry, towels and other soft goods (Burns, 1987; Mahar, 1987; Scacco, 1987). Both Euromonitor (1986), and the Direct Selling Education Foundation (1984) suggested and theoretically justified using various socioeconomic characteristics to explain the success of direct selling in the marketing of products cross culturally. Second, Economic theory supports the hypothesized relationship. In developing countries, direct selling may be filling distribution gaps which economists believe may act as barriers to economic development. Weber (1983) suggested that the Industry Market Potential (IMP) for each product line is in part a function of the size of the distribution gap which a firm faces in each country. Distribution gaps and other forms of market gaps inhibit products and services from reaching and penetrating potential markets, causing countries to be under served. Because such gaps are more prevalent in less developed economies than in more developed ones, the market gaps may be caused by the same socioeconomic factors used to determine a country's stage of economic development.

Based on the results of a transaction cost analysis, Anderson and Coughlan (1987) observed, "Americans are more likely to integrate the distribution channel in highly developed industrialized countries (Western Europe)." Anderson attributed the difference to cultural dissimilarity. It is possible, however, that the specific socioeconomic factors which influence channel integration decisions may be identifiable. Anderson and Coughlan also found that integration is directly related to the transaction specificity of assets. One might ask the extent to which a nation's socioeconomic characteristics determine if sales person training and experience will provide a sufficient return on investment. If the training and experience will not provide a sufficient return on investment, direct selling or some other form of nonintegrated channel will probably be established. One might expect training and experience to have their greatest payoffs in fully developed nations.

Slater et al. (1970), Riley et al. (1970), and Goldman (1974, 1975, 1981) developed theories which argue that a reduction in distribution gaps will cause economic development. They assert that the creation of high volume, low margin food (and other perishables) distribution systems will increase both consumer demand and producer productivity.

This paper argues that the use of direct selling may provide a method of meeting unsatisfied consumer demand in a market place which does not have the socio-economic capital necessary to develop adequate supermarket or department store space. The research provided in this paper is designed to identify the specific socio-economic characteristics which best explain the direct selling success. To test the hypothesis that the success of direct selling is related to specific national characteristics, a research methodology was developed.

RESEARCH METHODOLOGY

An after only design research methodology was used to determine if the success of direct selling is a function of specific socioeconomic characteristics. A longitudinal study was not undertaken due to time constraints and problems involving international exchange rates across time.

Cosmetics and fragrances are the products used in this study. However, based on the previously mentioned direct selling personnel observations, results should be generalizable to most consumer products. Other research method decisions concern sample selection, variable selection, and statistical methods selection. These are discussed below.

Sample Selection

The markets selected include those for which direct selling success data could be obtained. Because Avon Products was willing to supply these data, countries which Avon had entered or were considering for entry were used. The sample consisted of 32 countries, of which approximately twelve were mature, seven were newly industrialized and thirteen were developing. Although thirty two countries is not a large sample size by most statistical standards, recognize that it represents a fairly large proportion of the total nation population. The countries used in this study include Argentina, Australia, Austria, Belgium, Brazil, Canada, Chili, Columbia, Dominican Republic, France, Germany, Greece, Guatemala, Holland, Honduras, Italy, Japan, Malaysia, Mexico, New Zealand, Nigeria, Peru, Philippines, Portugal, Puerto Rico, Spain, Switzerland, Taiwan, Thailand, United Kingdom, United States, and Venezuela.

Dependent Variable Selection

To evaluate the viability of using direct selling as a method of marketing new products, Percentage of Market Potential (POM) is used as a measure of commercial success, and is similar to one of the measures of success defined during PDMA, 1991. In this paper, Percentage of Market Potential is different from market share. POM is defined in this study as the percentage of total sales attributed to the direct selling of products by every firm in the industry, regardless of distribution strategy used.

$$\text{POM} = \frac{\text{Total Industry Sales From Direct Selling}}{\text{Total Industry Sales (Direct Selling + Instore + Direct Mktg)}}$$

POM is used in this paper because it allows the researcher to evaluate the potential that direct selling offers when new products are launched in international markets.

Independent Variable Selection

Independent variables were selected in meetings with Avon Products international region management personnel. During the meetings, national characteristics thought to be related to direct selling success were identified based on either a literature search or personal observation. These data were then screened by two tests. First, the characteristics had to be either theoretically or logically justifiable. Characteristics which could not be supported by at least a logical argument, were eliminated from further consideration.

Second, the characteristics had to be obtainable through existing data bases. If a characteristic listed was not found in the data bases, surrogates were sought. If surrogates were unobtainable, the characteristic was deleted from the list. National character and cultural values are examples of characteristics which are not included in this study.

Because international data may vary from source to source, multiple sources of data were sought for each variable. Where differences were found to occur in the data, a selection was made based on either the perceived credibility and objectivity of the source, or the data are averaged. Sources of data included Euromonitors (for all parts of the world), Business International, Interpol, statistical abstracts (from United States, Tawain, France, Europe, and international), The U.N. Food and Agricultural Organization, the U.N. Demographic Yearbook, the World Development Report, World Economic Indicators, World Handbook of Political and Social Indicators, the World Bank, and the International Monetary Fund.

Variables selected for inclusion are: percent of household income spent on food and clothing, the extent to which income distribution is skewed, literacy rate, number of TV sets per capita, average age, private consumption income per capita, percent of population receiving mail at home, percent of population living in urban areas, trucks and buses in use per capita, percent of working women, and robbery/violent crime per capita.

Statistical Method Selection

Bivariate regression and correlation analyses are used to test the hypothesis that the POM obtainable from the direct selling of new products is related to socioeconomic characteristics taken one at a time. The socioeconomic characteristics used are shown in Table 1.

The socioeconomic characteristics found to explain the success of launching new products via direct selling were factor analyzed to obtain parsimony and to reduce multicollinearity.

Factor scores obtained from the factor analysis allow countries to be placed on a continuum. The continuum indicates the extent to which the countries vary across the selected socioeconomic characteristics. A similar procedure was used to define national power levels by Rummel (1968).

The proportion of the variance of the POM explained by socioeconomic characteristics was obtained by regressing the POM against the factor scores.

Internal validity was measured by using a jackknife procedure to determine the stability of the regression coefficients. A .05 level of significance was used for this test.

ANALYSIS AND RESULTS

Results of the bivariate correlation analysis are shown in Table 1. Because the sample sizes differ, a correlation matrix is not presented. The results indicate a 95% or greater probability that POM obtained from the direct selling of products is directly related to food as a percent of household income and the extent to which income distribution is skewed. It is inversely related to age, number of TV's per capita, literacy rate, private consumption income per capita, and

TABLE 1
BIVARIATE RELATIONSHIPS BETWEEN POM & SOCIOECONOMIC CHARACTERISTICS

PREDICTORS	SAMPLE SIZE	F VALUE	PROB (1 TAIL)	CORR COEFF
AVERAGE AGE OF POPULATION	28	36.9	<.001	-.760
NUMBER OF TV'S PER CAPITA	28	24.8	<.001	-.698
% LITERACY	28	22.0	<.001	-.677
FOOD AS A % OF HOUSEHOLD EXPENSE	27	20.7	<.001	.673
% INCOME HELD BY LOWEST 40% OF POPULATION	26	19.4	<.001	-.668
% INCOME HELD BY TOP 20% OF POPULATION	26	17.5	<.001	.650
% POPULATION HAVING MAIL DELIVERED AT HOME	15	9.4	.005	-.647
PRIVATE CONSUMPTION INCOME PER CAPITA	27	17.5	<.001	-.642
% POPULATION LIVING IN THE URBAN AREAS	28	4.4	.023	-.380
CLOTHING AS A % OF HOUSEHOLD EXPENSE	20	1.9	.091	.311
TRUCKS & BUSINESS IN USE PER CAPITA	28	1.8	.096	-.254
% OF WORKING WOMEN	28	.2	.321	-.092
ROBBERY AND VIOLENT CRIME PER CAPITA	19	.1	.389	-.069

percent of population living in urban areas. These results were in the expected tails.

Factor analysis was performed on eight of the socioeconomic characteristics, each with a sample size of at least twenty seven. These include age, number of TV's per capita, literacy rate, food expenditures as a percent of household income, private consumption income per capita, percentage of population living in urban areas, trucks and buses in use per capita, and percentage of working women.

Results of a varimax (orthogonal) factor analysis are shown in Table 2. Four factors were obtained. These were labeled "Consumer Wealth," "Consumer Urbanization and Literacy," "Percent Working Women," and "Infrastructure." The first two factors had eigenvalues equal or greater than 1.0, and accounted for 77% of the variance of the variables. The last two factors had eigenvalues equal to 0.8 and 0.4, and consisted of variables shown to be unrelated to direct selling POM. (See Tables 1 and 2.) Based on these eigenvalues and predetermined relationships, the researcher decided to use factor 1 and factor 2 in a subsequent multiple regression analysis.

Multiple regression analysis was performed to determine the extent to which the factor scores from factor 1 (Consumer Wealth) and factor 2 (Consumer Urbanization and literacy) could be used to explain the POM obtained from the direct selling of products. Results indicate that: (1) there is greater than a 99.9% chance of a relationship; and, (2) that 60% (adj. R^2) of the POM can be explained by the two factors. (Fifty-four percent is explained by factor 1 and six percent is explained by factor 2.) Both regression coefficients were significant at the .05 level.

The standardized regression coefficients indicate that consumer wealth (factor 1) is approximately 2.7 times more important in determining POM than is consumer urbanization and literacy (factor 2).

Nations with the smallest market gaps, mature nations such as Holland, Belgium, and Switzerland, provide the least potential.

To validate the regression model, a jackknife procedure was performed. Nine subsamples, taken in groups of three, were used.

Results of the validation of the regression equation indicate that the regression coefficient for factor 1 (consumer wealth) is stable

TABLE 2
Varimax Rotated Factor Matrix

	FACTOR 1 CONSUMER WEALTH	FACTOR 2 URBANIZATION AND LITERACY	FACTOR 3 % WORKING WOMEN	FACTOR 4 INFRA-STRUCTURE	COMMUNALITY
TV'S/CAP	.88919	.28832	.21229	.20866	.96239
INCOME/CAP	.82167	.26033	.22114	.36691	.92645
FOOD	-.80695	-.47635	.01956	-.15046	.89260
AGE (MEAN)	.79674	.39622	.27465	-.09228	.87573
URBAN	.35825	.85410	-.18589	.12745	.90863
LITERACY	.48622	.75883	.28902	.01361	.89595
WORKING WOMEN	.21904	-.01755	.94013	.16641	.95982
TRUCKS/ CAP	.16472	.07105	.14604	.95712	.96958
EIGENVALUES	4.93	1.23	.82	.41	
PCT OF VAR	61.6	15.4	10.3	5.1	
CUM PCT	61.6	77.0	87.2	92.4	

(Jackknife coefficient = -15.68, t value = -6.98, df = 8, P value < .001). The regression coefficient for factor 2 (consumer urbanization and literacy) may however be spurious (Jackknife coefficient = -6.78, t value = -1.18, df = 8, P value = .3).

In addition to the jackknife procedure, the regression equation was used to accurately predict the POM for Columbia and Greece. Observed POM data on Columbia and Greece surfaced only after a predicted POM was calculated. In both cases, the actual POM fell within a few percentage points of the expected. Although not a large hold out sample, the results are encouraging.

DISCUSSION

The prior analyses tested the hypothesis that direct selling success is a function of national characteristics. Results of the analyses indicate that this hypothesis should be accepted for consumer wealth and possibly for consumer urbanization and literacy.

Figure 1 compares the predicted to the observed POM's. The predicted values represent the economic development continuum on which the nations are placed by the two factor scores. The observed values indicate the extent to which the direct selling of products is successful in various nations.

The curve supports the theory discussed in the introduction of this paper. Nations with the largest market gaps, less developed nations such as Nigeria, Thailand and the Philippines, provide the greatest potential POM for the direct selling of new products.

These findings agree with O'Halloran, Hall, Barnes, Arnold, and Wilson's (1985) observation, that countries with lower levels of consumer wealth, such as Nigeria, Thailand and the Philippines, tend to have a higher proportion of product sales resulting from direct selling than do mature countries with higher levels of consumer wealth, such as Holland, Belgium, and Switzerland.

Firms interested in marketing products in foreign markets should evaluate the consumer wealth of those markets prior to deciding on a distribution method or on product features. If a country with low consumer wealth is the target market, then direct selling should be considered as a method of entry.

Most firms specialize in either in-store selling, direct marketing or direct selling when launching new products. This specialization may carry a lost opportunity cost. It is suggested that multinational firms become more flexible in their methods of distributing new products by learning to use marketing approaches not currently in their repertoires. Direct selling may, for instance, be a viable strategy for launching products into China, Eastern Europe, and/or the Commonwealth of Independent States. In-store distribution may be a more viable entry method in mature countries, such as those in Western Europe.

For firms not currently involved in direct selling, two tasks should be performed. First, the firms should either learn how to establish a direct selling distribution system or should partner with a firm which specializes in direct selling. And second, they should develop products which are amenable to direct selling. Products which are distributed by direct selling vary across subcultures or even national boundaries. This variation should not be perceived as an a priori suggestion that products sold via direct selling in one country may not be distributed by direct selling in another. The Japanese, for instance, use direct selling to market automobiles to potential customers. Automobiles are not the type of product that we, in the United States, normally think of as being amenable to direct selling. However, with an interesting blend of both direct selling and direct marketing, Amway is currently developing a domestic, discount buying club consisting of a multilevel direct selling network to distribute catalogs which may include automobiles. Products with one or more of the following features should lend themselves to direct selling:

1. The product has a high personal selling elasticity. Persuasion may be effective when selling products which customers might delay purchasing. Life insurance policies, magazine subscriptions, and encyclopedias are examples of products with such a characteristic. Even fur coats have been sold via direct selling.

2. The product is part of the home and benefits from the use of a demonstration in the home, or is a home improvement type item where home measurements have to be taken. Burglar alarms, water purification devices, replacement windows and siding are examples.

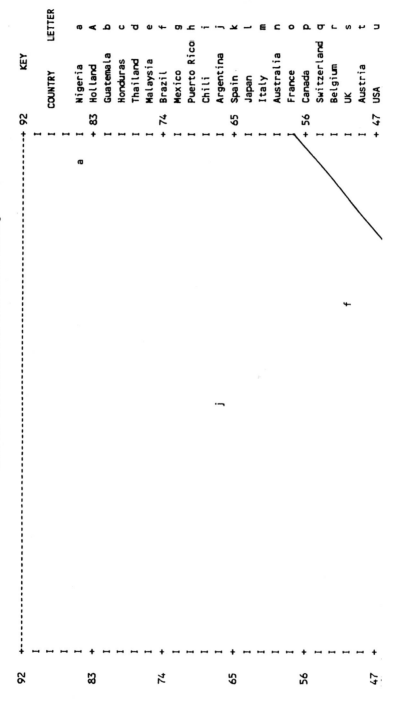

FIGURE 1
Observed vs Predicted POM from Direct-Selling

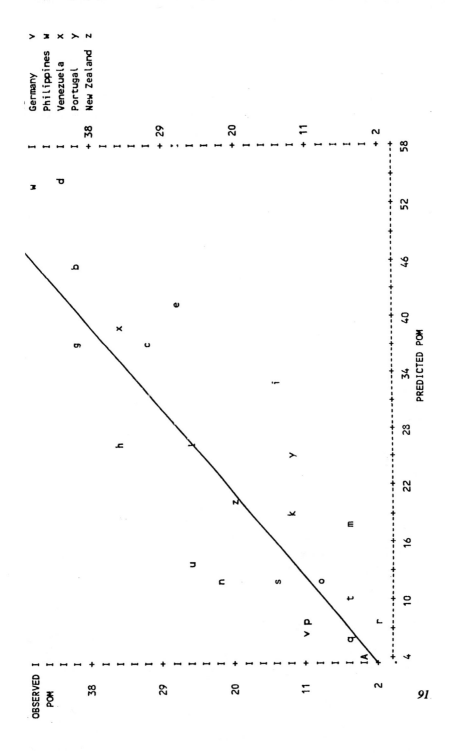

3. The product is one which benefits from demonstration, but is not part of the home. Towels, clothing, and other soft goods, food, cosmetics, perfumes and toiletries, cleaning supplies such as mops, brushes, vacuum cleaners, and detergents are examples.

4. The product is one which requires a private discussion. Examples include prearranged funerals and financial planning.

5. The product benefits from reference group interaction. The party plan selling of lingerie, jewelry, and kitchen gadgets are examples.

It is recognized that factors other than the socioeconomic indicators may also influence the percentage of market (POM) obtained from direct selling of new products. Anderson and Coughlan (1987), found that transaction specificity of assets and product differentiation level were directly related to integration of the distribution channels, which suggests that direct selling may work better when the transaction specificity and the level of differentiation are low. In addition, unexplained residuals shown in Figure 1 may be explained by measurement errors, other product characteristics (Mahar, 1987), business law, managerial effectiveness (Burns, 1987; Rogers, 1983), and national character (McClelland, 1961; De Vos, 1987). These measures may explain 40% or more of direct selling's percentage of market in this study, and therefore warrant future analysis.

REFERENCES

Anderson, Erin & Coughlan, Anne T. (1987), "International Market Entry and Expansion via Independent or Integrated Channels of Distribution," *Journal of Marketing*, Vol. 51 (pp 71-82).

Burns, J. Robert (1987), discussions with the President, Stanley Home Products.

De Vos, Richard M. (1987),"Direct Selling: the Human Equation in Marketing," Amway Corp.

Direct Selling Education Foundation (1984), Presentation to faculty at Brennon's Restaurant, New Orleans, (November).

Euromonitor (1986), "Direct Selling in the United Kingdom: The Market for Door-to-Door and Party Plan Selling 1980-1990," *Retail and Distribution Surveys,* Euromonitor, London.

Goldman, Arieh (1974), "Outreach of Consumers and the Modernization of Urban Food Retailing in Developing Countries," *Journal of Marketing*. Vol. 38 N4. Oct. PP. 8-16.

Goldman, Arieh (1975), "The Role of Trading-Up in the Development of the Retailing System," *Journal of Marketing,* Vol.39 N1. Jan. PP. 54-62.

Goldman, Arieh (1981), "Transfer of Retailing Technology into the Less Developed Countries: The Supermarket Case," *Journal of Retailing,* Vol. 57 N2, Summer, PP. 5-29.

Linen, C.T. (1991), "Marketing And The Global Economy," *Direct Marketing,* January, PP. 54-56.

Mahar, Lawrence J. (1987), discussion with Encyclopedia Britannica Inc.'s Vice President, International.

McClelland, David C. (1961), *The Achieving Society*; Princeton: D. Van Nostrand.

PDMA Success/Failure Task Force Meeting, April 4, 1991.

O'Halloran, Colin, Sharon Hall, Ted Barnes, David Arnold, and Donna Wilson (1985), discussions with Avon Corp.'s Directors of Strategic Planning for Latin America, the Pacific Basin, and Europe.

Pickholz, J.W. (1988), "The End Of The World (As We Know It)," *Direct Marketing,* Sept., pp. 42-45.

Rapp, Stan (1989), "The 'directmarketization' of the world," *Direct Marketing,* November, PP. 78, 99.

Rapp, Stan & Collins, Tom, (1990), *The Great Marketing Turnaround, The Age of the Individual and How to Profit From It*; Prentice Hall Inc.

Rogers, Everett M. (1983), *Diffusion of Innovations* 3rd Edition The Free Press.

Riley, Harold, C. Slater, K. Harrison, J. Wish, J. Griggs, V. Farace J. Santiago, I. Rodriguez (1970), *Food Marketing in the Economic Development of Puerto Rico,* Research Report No. 4, Latin American Studies Center, Michigan State University.

Rummel, R.J. (1968), "Understanding Factor Analysis" an invited paper for *The Journal of Conflict Resolution.*

Sanghavi, N. (1988), "International 800–An Update on New Strategic Initiatives," *Direct Marketing,* April, p. 42.

Scacco, Peter (1987), discussions with Amway's Director of International Public Relations.

Slater, Charles, H. Riley, V. Farace, K. Harrison, F. Neves, A. Bogatay, M. Doctoroff, D. Larson, R. Nason, T. Webb (1970), *Marketing Processes in the Recife Area of Northeast Brazil,* Research Report No. 2, Latin American Studies Center, Michigan State University.

Weber, John A. (1983), "International Market Structure Profile Analysis: A Systematic Approach to Assessing Growth Opportunities in the International Marketplace" in *International Marketing,* Third Edition by Vern Terpstra; Dryden Press; p. 571-579.

Wunderman, Lester (1986), "Wunderman's View of Global Direct Marketing," *Direct Marketing,* March, pp. 76-78, 80, 82, 86, 88, 153.

Current Status and Future Directions for Research on Direct Selling Channels

Gerald Albaum

SUMMARY. Direct selling is not a new method of distribution. It has a rich history. But, until the late 1980s there was a paucity of published empirical research on direct selling. This paper reviews, in a descriptive way, the research that has been done since the mid-1980s on both the sales side and consumer side of this method of distribution. In addition, a survey of executives of direct selling companies was conducted to assess whether researchers have been studying the major problems faced by direct sellers. It appears that there is a poor match between those problems perceived as most important by practitioners and the problems studied by academicians.

INTRODUCTION

Non-store retailing has generated considerable research interest in recent years, primarily due to its phenomenal growth. Industry statistics reveal non-store retailing is growing at a rate more than double that of in-store retailing. Most of the published empirical research on non-store retailing has focused on in-home shoppers–consumers who purchase merchandise by telephone, computer, or catalog from their home (Berkowitz, Walton, & Walker, 1979; Cunningham & Cunningham, 1973; Darian, 1987; Gillette, 1976; Sharma, Bearden, & Teel, 1983). Recently, there have been two articles on what the future might hold for some types of non-store retailing

---

Gerald Albaum is Professor of Marketing, University of Oregon and Senior Research Fellow, IC[2] Institute, University of Texas at Austin.

95

(Achabol & McIntyre, 1992; Schultz, 1992). Technology advances will provide retailers of all types with substantial opportunities and challenges. For example, as we move into the 21st century, interactive home-based systems that integrate the personal computer, telephone, and high definition television (HDTV) are expected to provide more alternatives to fixed-location retailing, and the percentages of purchases via home-based shopping will increase several-fold (Achabol & McIntyre, 1992). Schultz (1992) goes even further with his predictions and states that the day of the traditional fixed-location retailer is limited. He predicts that retailing will become direct/database marketing and direct/database marketing will become retailing.[1]

Until the late 1980s there was a paucity of published research on one of the most common, yet unique, forms of non-store retailing, *direct selling*. In their review of what empirical research had been published Albaum and Peterson (1989) reported that for the most part, the retailing literature, both academic and trade, virtually ignored direct selling, despite its rich history (e.g., the Yankee peddler). To illustrate, an extensive review of *Journal of Retailing* issues through 1988 revealed only *two* published articles on direct selling in the previous 50 years: a descriptive appraisal of the industry (Granfield & Nicols, 1975) and an examination of "cooling-off" laws in Arizona (Tootelian, 1975). Moreover, despite a comprehensive literature search, only one article (Peters & Ford, 1972) and one book (Jolson, 1970) were found that reported empirical research on consumers who purchase from direct sales companies. Albaum and Peterson (1989) provided an overview of empirical research on direct selling that became available in the last half of the 1980s. Most of the research they reported on were studies available as unpublished working papers. Some of these have since been published in journals.

The year 1988 seems to have been a pivotal year for empirical research on direct selling. Starting then, there have been almost one dozen published studies and a number of unpublished working papers. The need for empirical research on all aspects of direct selling now is greater than ever as we move toward the year 2000. Wotruba (1992) has stated that as direct selling approaches the year 2000, it faces some major challenges in its customer market and its labor market. These challenges carry over into management issues–managing the sales force and sales operations and "managing" markets. Individual direct sales companies, particularly the larger ones (e.g., Avon, Tupperware, etc.) do marketing and market research. Their studies, however, typically are proprietary and are not generally available to other companies in the industry. Since the major challenges facing the industry are general and cross product lines and affect companies of all sizes, there is need for the kinds of research that academic researchers do and are well suited for.

The purpose of this article is to provide an overview of the recent empirical research on direct selling. As such, then, it represents an extension of the review by Albaum and Peterson (1989), and brings that study up-to-date. But the present paper goes further. An attempt is made to answer the question, "Are empirical researchers concerned with the same issues and challenges that practitioners are?" To answer this question a survey was conducted of managers within the industry that asked them to identify the major problems facing the industry and the major problems facing their companies. If we researchers are not studying the phenomena that managers feel are important problem areas then there is need to reexamine the dialogue between practitioners and academics that is taking place or is failing to take place.

WHAT IS DIRECT SELLING?

Direct selling is defined by the Direct Selling Association as "personal contact between a salesperson and a consumer away from a fixed business location such as a retail store" (Bernstein & Associates, 1984, p. 4). Major modes of direct selling include one-on-one selling in a home, one-on-one selling at a workplace, sales party at a consumer's home, and sales party at a workplace, church, or other location. In 1991 direct selling revenues totaled approximately $13.0 billion in the United States, and the industry employed more than 5.0 million individuals as sales representatives in the United States (Direct Selling Association, 1992).[2] In 1991, sales of direct selling companies in 16 countries of Europe were about $6.6 billion, and this was achieved by 1.3 million salespeople (European

Federation of Direct Selling Association, 1992). Estimates of worldwide direct sales activity show that more than 9 million salespeople produced sales of about $40.2 million in 32 countries in 1989 (World Federation of Direct Selling Associations, 1990). Although the industry in the United States, and other countries as well, is populated by relatively small firms and firms (large and small) that are not well known (e.g., Princess House, Vorwerk, Noevir, Diamite, Home Interiors and Gifts, Jafra), several firms are household names, including Avon, Amway, Tupperware, Encyclopedia Britannica, Electrolux, Mary Kay, Fuller Brush, and Herbalife. Products sold vary widely (e.g., cosmetics, vitamins, reference books, cutlery, vacuum cleaners, clothing, cleaning products, kitchenware, toys/crafts, hobbies, hand tools, etc.) and cover a wide range of prices.

Although both the industry and the majority of direct selling companies are relatively small, nearly every household in the United States has purchased something from a company using this method of distribution. Peterson, Albaum, and Ridgway (1989) report that 92 percent of the individuals questioned in a national survey had purchased at least once in their adult lifetime from a direct sales company, and 57 percent stated they had made such a purchase within the 12-month period prior to data collection. Given the number of consumers who have purchased from a direct sales firm, it is important that there be more empirical research conducted and reported, including descriptive research. Such research can serve as a baseline for future studies on consumer purchasing behavior and, in addition, can provide insights for both in-store and non-store retailers.

MAJOR MANAGEMENT ISSUES IN DIRECT SELLING

Two major areas of managerial concern in direct selling are the company itself or the *selling side,* and the market or the *consumer side.* To provide a perspective on this research, illustrative studies are highlighted below. There is no attempt made to give a thorough review of the findings of this body of knowledge either by a meta analysis involving a quantitative review (Wolf, 1986) or by the more traditional approaches to literature reviews. Rather, what follows is a brief discussion of the nature of those studies covered by this review. There is not a sufficiently large number of studies nor do there appear to be streams of research that are programmatic such that a traditional review or meta analysis would be revealing of anything beyond looking at each study itself. In short, the situation is that there does not yet exist a body of knowledge that needs to be "tied together" for the purpose of understanding what direct selling is all about.

Although each study has been categorized as studying some issue(s) of either the selling or customer sides, there are some studies that deal with both areas of concern. These have been included where it appears their major contribution lies, if this can be determined. If not, it is discussed in both areas. Since not every direct selling research study is included in this review, no claim is made for the exhaustiveness of the investigation. However, most of the major research studies are included, and there is no reason to believe that the articles and papers included do not constitute a representative and comprehensive sampling of the relevant literature on direct selling. These studies are sufficient for examining the question of whether researchers have been studying the problem areas of most importance to direct sales practitioners.

The Selling Side of Direct Sales

Research pertaining to the selling side of direct sales has ranged from being broadly focused to investigating specific aspects of the direct selling process and management of the sales operations of companies.

On a more or less annual basis, the Direct Selling Association conducts a study which has three objectives: (a) estimating the total U.S. retail sales of direct sales companies, (b) determining the total number of salespeople involved in direct selling, and (c) providing basic information on industry practices. Both Association member companies and nonmember firms are surveyed to obtain the necessary data. Industry projections are then made based on responses received. Similar quantitative data for worldwide direct selling activities are published by the Worldwide Federation of Direct Selling Associations.

One of the first broad-based studies is by Enis (1986). In this study, discussions were held with the chief executive officer of a number of direct sales companies regarding selected management issues and concerns. The study focused on changing consumer and selling trends that will significantly affect direct selling companies in the immediate future. The study was concerned with the four major "players" in the industry–customers, sales representatives, companies, and society.

A more recent broad-based study was conducted by Eleanor May (1991). In this study direct selling is viewed as a unique channel of distribution for consumer goods, as compared with other forms of retailing. The emphasis is on changes that have occurred and are occurring, in the marketplace, and what the future may hold. The purpose of the study is to assess whether direct selling can survive as a channel of distribution for consumer goods and what actions may be needed to preserve it. The empirical findings are based on interviews with 22 executives from 12 companies and a mail survey of 550 salesforce representatives from 11 companies which resulted in responses from 266 sales representatives. Although consumers are discussed, the emphasis clearly is on the selling side and on major aspect of "managing" the salesforce. One overall conclusion reached is that the future of direct selling in the United States is uncertain, and much will depend on the maintenance of the *entrepreneurial spirit* which seems to be essential to success in direct selling.

In an unpublished paper, Cravens, Ingram, LaForge, and Young (1990) report on a survey of the chief sales executives from 25 direct selling companies. The average salesforce size for these companies is about 30,000, and the average sales revenue per salesperson is $220,000. The results presented in the paper summarize the practices and priorities of the non-probability-selected sample companies. Selling and sales management activities are described and no normative statements are made. The study examines the selling characteristics of the markets served by the companies, the frequency of 11 selling activities performed by salespeople, sales management control systems used, activities of field sales managers, salesperson performance, and sales organization performance. The data in this study present a profile about selling and sales management practices. As such, these findings may be used as benchmarks, or reference guidelines, by companies wanting to examine their own behaviors.

As mentioned earlier, technology is of concern to the industry. One potentially useful tool direct sales companies might be able to use is *videotex*, which is a generic term for a developing, interactive medium that delivers text and visual information directly to consumers. It has the potential to reach either mass or tightly targeted audiences in both home and business markets. In the early 1980s, Talarzyk and Widing (1982a, b) studied videotex and its implications for marketing.

A somewhat intriguing aspect of direct selling was addressed in a study by Thistlethwaite, Norvell, Kornendowski, Billingsley, and Epperson (1984). The purpose of this study was to describe the practice of direct selling in a small midwestern town. The researchers were especially interested in studying such issues as the types of people involved in direct selling, what initially motivates them to become direct sellers and continue to sell over time, and what it would take to recruit other individuals to become direct sellers. Unfortunately, the study does not permit broad generalizations because data were collected in a single location. Also concerned with kinds of people attracted to direct selling is the study by Crawford and Garland (1988). This published study presented the results of a nationwide survey of female party plan sales forces and looks at what kinds of people are attracted to party plan selling and whether there are significant life-style differences between those sales people who look upon what they do as a career and those who do it simply to make extra money.

A major research effort has examined the sales force turnover problem (Wotruba, 1990a, b, 1991). This body of research has sought to assess what affects turnover among direct salespeople. Examined were the effects of job satisfaction, job performance, job image (i.e., salespeople's perception of the public image of selling), and met expectations. Comparisons between part-time and full-time salespeople are included in this research effort, as are comparisons between active and inactive direct salespeople. This stream of research is based on a mail survey of 1600 salespeople throughout the United States who are associated with one of four direct selling companies. Usable responses were obtained from almost 500 sales-people. Most of the respondents were female with a median age of 27 and median education of some college. Findings emerging from this research are that part-time salespeople (i.e., those with other jobs at the same time) have greater job satisfaction and less propensity to quit than full-time salespeople, salespeople with more negative perception of the public image of their job tend to have lower job satisfaction and tend to be more prone to inactivity, and met expectations influences whether direct salespeople stay or leave their sales job. Since turnover in direct selling typically is voluntary and often very high, companies face a major problem having great cost. Therefore, the more that is known about the causes and consequences of salesforce turnover the better companies will be able to manage it.[3]

Related to the issues of salesperson turnover and job satisfaction is motivating salespeople to perform. Beltramini and Evans (1988) examine the role of sales contests for such purposes. This research is based on a mail survey of 2,000 salespersons from three direct sales companies. Usable responses were received from 933 sales-people, with approximately one-half of these reporting their performance to be in the top 30 percent of the salespeople in their company. Conclusions reached in this research suggest that while sales contests are a potentially useful motivation device, to be used as short-term motivators, they should be perceived by salespersons as separate from compensation. The reason for this is that there is some evidence that contests become the principal (if not sole) source of motivation for some salespeople–i.e., they sit and wait for certain contests which offer rewards of interest to them.

Other areas of research interest on the selling side include the effect of goal-setting on the performance of independent contractors (Wotruba, 1989), what can be done to help sales representatives obtain repeat sales, increase customer retention, and obtain new customers (Raymond, 1990), and the dynamics of the party plan approach to direct selling (Belch & Swasy, 1991).

It is clear from the above exposition that there is no pattern to the research stream on the selling side of direct selling. What we see is a collection of individual studies which are largely unrelated to each other. One topic where there have been multiple articles published is salesforce turnover. But, this research is based on a single data set. This situation is not particularly surprising as serious researcher interest in the problems facing direct selling companies and the method of distribution did not start until the late 1980s.

The Consumer Side of Direct Sales

General knowledge about the consumer which has been widely disseminated in the industry stems from two studies, both of which are now dated. The first was conducted for the Direct Selling Association in 1976 by Louis Harris and Associates (Direct Selling Association, 1977). A total of 18 product categories were investigated. The objective of the study was to assess attitudes toward the direct selling industry, focusing on its strengths and weaknesses. Some six years later the Nowland Organization (1982) did a study for the Direct Selling Education Foundation. The objectives of this study were to update the Harris study and obtain specific information on three major segments of direct selling—repetitive person-to-person, non-repetitive person-to-person, and party plan.

One of the first of the "new wave" studies of the consumer side of direct selling is that of Peterson, Albaum, and Ridgway (1989). This study partially up-dates the Harris (Direct Selling Association, 1977) and Nowland (1982) studies on selected consumer-related issues. Excluded from this study is the individual who is simultaneously a salesperson/customer—that is, the salesperson who essentially buys for his/her own purposes and does not sell to others. The Peterson, Albaum, and Ridgway (1989) study sought to:

1. Determine the extent to which consumers buy from direct sales companies and document the demographic characteristics of purchasers and nonpurchasers.
2. Obtain perceptions of the advantages and disadvantages of buying from a direct sales company.
3. Investigate the perceived risk of buying from a direct sales company, as compared to buying through other modes of retail selling.

The research is descriptive and is based on a national sample of 1,600 consumers drawn from a national consumer mail panel. The 988 people responding are viewed as representing middle-class America.

Similar type data were obtained from 492 people in the study by Raymond (1990) that was briefly discussed in the previous section. Since the sample of consumers used by her was provided by participating direct selling companies, findings are not directly comparable to those of Peterson, Albaum, and Ridgway (1989). Moreover, Raymond's (1990) study examined other issues as well–incentives for repeat purchasing and for increasing order size and improvements consumers would like to see in direct selling companies.

A study by Barnowe and McNabb (1988) in the Pacific Northwest investigated consumer experiences with, and attitudes toward, direct selling methods. Specifically, this study profiled demographic, attitudinal, and psychographic differences between individuals who either purchase or do not purchase from direct sales companies. Also explored were overall attitudes toward alternative sales methods, perceived advantages and disadvantages of direct selling, and potential improvements in direct selling methods that would make direct selling experiences more attractive and satisfying to consumers. Data were obtained from 491 households in three metropolitan areas by personal interview.

The most recent broad-based study from the consumers' perspective also looks at how a company might best integrate one or more direct marketing techniques–e.g., direct mail or telemarketing–with its direct sales operation (Massey & Seitz, 1991). A mail survey of 4,000 U.S. households was conducted resulting in responses from 1,100 purchasers and non-purchasers of direct selling companies. The original sample was provided by direct selling companies and included active and inactive customers. The study investigated purchasing and shopping behavior, generalized orientation toward buying beliefs associated with direct selling, attitudes toward direct selling programs, and perceived satisfaction among users of this method of distribution.

An interesting observation can be made about the three studies just discussed (Massey & Seitz, 1991; Peterson, Albaum, & Ridgway, 1989; Raymond, 1990). Although they vary in comprehensiveness and breadth they do have considerable overlap. Yet, there are no cross-references among them. It is as if there is a stream of research but everyone is crossing the river at a different place. What seems to be lacking is a tradition for building on others' work, which is a sign of an "immature" research stream.

In a major study of in-home shopping needs of mature consumers (defined as being 65 or older), Lumpkin, Caballero, and Chonko (1989) examined the shopping behavior of these consumers with regard to direct selling and direct sellers. Included in the original sample of 4,000 drawn from a national mail panel were mature consumers, and consumers in two other age groups–21-54, 55-64–that were included for comparison purposes. Since the mature consumer group was disproportionately sampled, the sample is not representative. Based on responses from 2,500 people nationwide, the study examined the various physical, economic, and psychological needs of the mature consumer when shopping and looked at the question of whether these needs were being met by in-home shopping. Regarding direct selling and direct sellers, focus is placed on consumer attitudes. Willingness to purchase by this method of in-home shopping and consumer perceptions about the alternative modes of direct selling are examined.

Another area of research interest has been consumers involvement with the party plan method of direct selling. Raymond (1990) looked at descriptive aspects such as average number of guests attending, incentives offered to get others to host a party and to help in booking more parties, places where parties are held, and reasons why people volunteer to host a party. More depth about why consumers decide to attend and purchase at home parties is provided by Frenzen and Davis (1989). Specifically, the following types of data were obtained in the Chicago area from people attending parties for personal care products:

1. Usage rate and brand preferences of the product category.
2. Travel time to a party and to the retail store where personal care products were normally purchased.
3. Social relationships between hostess and guests and between guests and the sales representative.
4. Amount purchased at the party.
5. Prior home party attendance.

These two researchers have used the party plan mode of direct selling as an application of more general phenomena in consumer and buyer behavior. In one study they explored the concept of ascription as it operates in consumer markets (Davis & Frenzen, 1986). Ascription is defined as the process whereby one organization makes use of a second organization for its own purposes. In the case of the party-plan company, it uses the social network underlying the party in order to gain low-cost access to a consumer market. It is argued that companies using the party plan method utilize existing social relationships to access demand and successfully overcome the related problems of network access, engagement, and disengagement. All tasks are transferred to the hostess by the company:

1. Access–the hostess invites people.
2. Engagement–the "party" is used as a pretext to get the people to a specific place.
3. Disengagement–all orders are technically placed by the hostess and are delivered to the hostess, who is responsible for delivery, etc.

Using data from 96 parties held by one company selling women's clothing, it was found that in addition to economic forces of effective price, demand is also driven by the existing store of social indebtedness among consumers.

The last study of the party plan method to be discussed is one which examined the concept of market embeddedness and its impact on purchasing behavior in a consumer market (Frenzen & Davis, 1990). Embeddedness exists when consumers simultaneously derive utility from two sources–attributes of the product, and social capital found in pre-existing ties between buyers and sellers. This line of research is based on earlier work by James Davis (1973) who suggested that the home party method of direct sales would be a good vehicle for studying the impact of social relations on market transactions and work by Taylor (1978) who concluded, based largely on anecdotal evidence, that home party companies co-opted social relations among women who agree to host home parties and their invitees. Frenzen and Davis (1990) used self-report survey techniques to obtain data from a sample of hostesses and their invitees attending parties for personal care products in the Chicago area. It is concluded that the degree of social capital present, as measured by the buyer-seller tie strength and buyer indebtedness to the seller, significantly increases the likelihood of purchase at home parties.

Unlike the situation that exists for the selling side of direct sales, there do appear to be research streams being developed within the consumer side. The work by Davis and Frenzen (1986) and Frenzen and Davis (1989, 1990) on party plans represents one such stream. In addition, the studies by Massey and Seitz (1991), Peterson, Albaum, and Ridgway (1989), and Raymond (1990) also can be viewed as a stream even though the researchers themselves have not recognized it as such.

IS THE RESEARCH USEFUL?

In addition to satisfying their own intellectual curiosity, academic researchers engage in their research with the expectation that some outside constituency will find the results useful. In an attempt to see if this holds for the research on direct selling, a small survey, using mail techniques, was conducted among direct sales company executives. The sample was provided by the Direct Selling Association (DSA) and included member company executives, members of the DSA board of directors, and members of the board of directors of the Direct Selling Education Foundation. Due to board memberships, some companies had more than one person in the original sample. The sample must be viewed, then, as that of individuals active in the industry, not companies. A total of 109 questionnaires were sent and usable responses were received from 27 executives, representing a 24.8% response rate. One follow-up was used. Respondents include board chairmen, presidents, vice presidents, sales managers, and other managers. Product lines represented are household products, cosmetics/skin care, cookware and cutlery, home decorative products, nutrition and food, books/magazines, large ticket items, and women's clothing. Although the obtained sample is not large in number it does seem to cover a "representative" range of products.

A necessary, but not sufficient, condition for academic research to be useful to managers is that they have read the research. At the very least they need to be aware that such research exists. Members of the sample were asked about their experiences with academic research on issues relevant to the direct selling industry that have been published in journals or as working papers by the Direct Selling Education Foundation. About 62.5% of responding executives stated they have read at least one such study, 29.2% report that they have heard such studies exist but have not read any, and only 8.3% are not familiar with the research.

But, does the research cover topics that are of interest to managers in the industry? Two questions were asked in this survey that address this question:

1. What are the three most important issues facing direct sellers in general (i.e., the industry) today?
2. What are the three most important problems facing your company today in its direct selling operations?

As might be expected, many respondents cited the same problem area both for the industry as a whole and for their company. This seems to indicate that executives feel their company's products are tied directly to what is happening in, and to, the industry.

Regarding the problems facing the industry more than 20 different types of problems were reported. Table 1 presents the problem areas that received mention by at least three respondents. Major problems identified by at least 20 percent of respondents are legal/regulatory issues, unethical behavior by companies that seem to "come and go," the status of the independent contractor system, recruiting/turnover of the sales force, and the overall image of direct sales per se. It is clear that the legal/regulatory/government area is by far the one that seems to be of concern to more executives than any other. The concern over the status of the independent contractor typically is over the legal status and its impact on taxation.

Turning now to managers' beliefs about the problems facing their companies, a more diverse pattern of responses was reported. Some 30 distinct problem areas were mentioned. Those areas mentioned by at least three respondents are shown in Table 2. As shown, there is less agreement among respondents regarding company-

TABLE 1

Manager's Perceptions of Problems Facing the Direct Selling Industry

Problem	Number of Respondent Indicating	Percent of All Respondents (N=27)
Legal/regulatory issues	19	55.6
Recruiting/turnover	11	40.7
Unethical behavior	10	37.0
Status of independent contractor system	9	33.3
Overall image of direct sales	7	25.9
Socio/demographic changes in the marketplace	4	14.8
Taxation	3	11.1
Access to potential customers	3	11.1

TABLE 2

Managers' Perceptions of Problem Faced by Their Companies

Problem	Number of Respondent Indicating	Percent of All Respondents (N=27)
Recruiting	15	55.6
Maintaining independent contractor status	5	18.5
Negative image of distribution method	4	14.8
Communications and administration within companies	4	14.8
New customer attraction	4	14.8
Managing growth	3	11.1
Retaining distributors	3	11.1
Finding good products at good prices	3	11.1

faced problems than there was for problems confronting the industry. The four most frequently mentioned problems are recruiting/turnover, maintaining the independent contractor status, the negative image of direct selling, and problems of communication, etc., in managing the company.

With the exception of recruiting/turnover, there does not seem to be much of a match between the research interests of academic researchers and the problems facing direct selling and direct sellers. Recruiting, and retaining distributors as well, is covered within the domain of salesforce turnover. In addition there is somewhat a match between the research stream on the customer side of direct sales and concern for problems involved in the changing marketplace, access to potential customers, and new customer attraction. But, the legal environment and the situation facing the status of the independent contractor system have been largely ignored by researchers. Similarly, issues of ethical behavior and the negative image held by the public also have been left alone. While it is not within the scope of this article to suggest how these important problems might be transformed into research questions, it is noteworthy that the major area of concern to those in the industry are not of equal interest to the academic researchers that have shown some intellectual curiosity about direct selling and direct sellers.

WHERE NOW?

Where do we go from here? It seems reasonable to conclude that the academic community has had little regard for direct selling as an area of intellectual and research interest. This may be due to the negative image of the industry alleged to be held by academics, or it may be due to a lack of awareness and knowledge of the industry and its economic impact. Still another reason for lack of interest may be the fact that the vast number of companies are relatively small and often considered to be nonreceptive to academic research. Regardless of the reason, direct selling has not been viewed as an "exciting" industry, one that deserves the attention of the academic community.

It is also clear that research on direct selling to date can be characterized as ad hoc in nature and as consisting of isolated studies that do not build upon each other. While there is a need for ad hoc studies, there is an even greater need for programmatic research. However, before this can happen in any meaningful way, there must be a dialogue between academics and direct selling practitioners. There exists what Bonoma (1988) has called an academic-practitioner gap. Because of this gap, the academic community does not know what industry needs and interests are, whereas practitioners do not know what academics have to offer.

Albaum and Peterson (1989) have proposed a model for practitioner/academic interactions. The traditional model is shown in Part A of Figure 1. Problems flow from practitioners to academics; research flows from academics to practitioners. All flows are one-way. A two-way flow is proposed (Part B of Figure 1) wherein a dialogue is established between practitioners and academics. Both problems and research move two ways, and it is through the dialogue that additional knowledge is generated and disseminated.

This dialogue will not occur by itself. Both sides have to take a first step. Ultimately, it is necessary that the dialogue be institutionalized. This means, in turn, that some type of clearinghouse is needed if institutionalization is to be effective. A professional association, such as the American Marketing Association or the Academy of Marketing Science, is in a somewhat unique position to act as such a clearinghouse since it can offer either periodic or on-going forums. Other possible clearinghouses would be more industry-based, e.g., the Direct Selling Education Foundation and/or the Direct Selling Association.

Only when practitioners and academics have a forum for their dialogue will knowledge be efficiently generated and disseminated.

FIGURE 1. Models of Practitioner/Academician Interaction

(A) Traditional Model

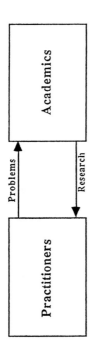

(B) Proposed Model

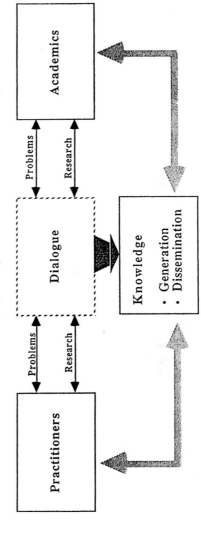

Source: Adapted from Albaum and Peterson (1989).

NOTES

1. Direct marketing is defined as "an interactive system of marketing which uses one or more advertising media to effect a measurable response and/or transaction at any location" (Stone, 1988, p. 3). Database marketing involves the creation of a large computerized file (database) of customers' and potential customers' profiles and purchase patterns and the use of this file to develop more specific, effective, and efficient marketing programs (Lamb, Hair, & McDaniel, 1992, p. 174; Schultz, 1992, p. 116).

2. Although often referred to as an industry, direct selling is more properly a method of marketing and distribution. Direct sales companies sell door-to-door, through parties, and increasingly through "over-the-counter" operations. It is important to note that the estimates do *not* include sales of services such as insurance and chimney cleaning or products such as home siding or Girl Scout cookies.

3. Although not exclusively concerned with direct salespeople, they were included in a study by Jolson, Dubinsky, & Anderson (1987) of 80 possible correlates of sales force tenure.

REFERENCES

Achabol, D., & McIntyre, S. (1992). Emerging technology in retailing: Challenges and opportunities for the 1990s. In R. A. Peterson (Ed.), *The future of U.S. retailing: An agenda for the 21st century* (pp. 85-128). New York: Quorum Books.

Albaum, G., & Peterson, R. A. (1989). *An overview of empirical research on direct selling.* Paper presented at the Annual Conference of the Academy of Marketing Science, Orlando, FL.

Barnowe, T., & McNabb, D. E. (1988). *The in-home shopper: Segmenting the direct selling market.* Unpublished working paper, Direct Selling Education Foundation, Washington, DC.

Belch, G. E., & Swasy, J. L. (1991). *The social influence dynamics of a party plan selling approach.* Unpublished working paper, Direct Selling Education Foundation, Washington, DC.

Beltramini, R. F., & Evans, K. R. (1988). Salesperson motivation to perform and job satisfaction: A sales contest participant perspective. *Journal of Personal Selling and Sales Management, 8*(2), 35-42.

Berkowitz, E. N., Walton, J. R., & Walker, O. C., Jr. (1979). In-home shoppers: The market for innovative distribution systems. *Journal of Retailing, 55,* 15-33.

Bernstein, R. A., & Associates. (1984). *Successful direct selling.* Englewood Cliffs, NJ: Prentice-Hall Inc.

Bonoma, T. V. (1988, November 21). Bridge builders needed on strategy. *Marketing News, 22,* 8.

Cravens, D. W., Ingram, T. N., LaForge, R. W., & Young, C. (1990). *Survey of selling priorities and sales management practices.* Unpublished working paper, Direct Selling Education Foundation, Washington, DC.

Crawford, J. C., & Garland, B. C. (1988). A profile of a party plan sales force. *Akron Business and Economic Review, 19*(4), 28-37.

Cunningham, I. C. M., & Cunningham, W. H. (1973). The urban in-home shopper: Socio-economic and attitudinal characteristics. *Journal of Retailing, 49,* 42-50.

Darian, J. C. (1987). In-home shopping: Are there customer segments? *Journal of Retailing, 63,* 163-186.

Davis, H. L., & Frenzen, J. (1986). *Neighborhoods, social networks, and market access.* Unpublished working paper, Direct Selling Education Foundation, Washington, DC.

Davis, J. (1973). Forms and norms: The economy of social relations. *Man, 8,* 159-176.

Direct Selling Association. (1977). *Highlights of a comprehensive survey of the direct selling industry.* Washington, DC: Direct Selling Association.

Direct Selling Association. (1992). *Direct selling growth and outlook mini-survey.* Washington, DC: Direct Selling Association.

Enis, B. (1986). *The direct selling industry: A systematic appraisal of future management issues.* Unpublished working paper, Direct Selling Education Foundation, Washington, DC.

European Federation of Direct Selling Association. (1992). *Annual report for 1991.* Brussels, Belgium: Author.

Frenzen, J. K., & Davis, H. L. (1989). *Consumer motivations to attend and buy at home parties.* Unpublished working paper, Direct Selling Education Foundation, Washington, DC.

Frenzen, J. K., & Davis, H. L. (1990). Purchasing behavior in embedded markets. *Journal of Consumer Behavior, 17*(1), 1-12.

Gillette, P. L. (1976). In-home shoppers: An overview. *Journal of Marketing, 40,* 81-88.

Granfield, M., & Nichols, A. (1975). Economic and marketing aspects of the direct selling industry. *Journal of Retailing, 51,* 33-49.

Jolson, M. A. (1970). *Consumer attitudes toward direct-to-home marketing systems.* New York: Dunellen.

Jolson, M. A., Dubinsky, A. J., & Anderson, R. E. (1987). Correlates and determinants of sales force tenure: An exploratory study. *Journal of Personal Selling and Sales Management, 7,* 9-27.

Lamb, C. W., Jr., Hair, J. F., Jr., & McDaniel, C. (1992). *Principles of marketing.* Cincinnati, OH: South-Western.

Lumpkin, J. R., Caballero, M. J., & Chonko, L. B. (1989). *Direct marketing, direct selling, and the mature consumer.* New York: Quorum Books.

Massey, T. K., Jr., & Seitz, V. A. (1991). *Melding complementary channels of distribution to support traditional direct selling efforts.* Unpublished working paper, Direct Selling Education Foundation, Washington, DC.

May, E. G. (1991). *Direct selling: A unique channel of distribution.* Unpublished working paper, Direct Selling Education Foundation, Washington, DC.

Nowland Corporation. (1982). *Consumer experiences and attitudes with respect to direct selling: A two-phase study.* Study prepared for the Direct Selling Education Foundation, Washington, DC.

Peters, W. H., & Ford, N. M. (1972). A profile of urban in-home shoppers: The other half. *Journal of Marketing, 36,* 62-64.

Peterson, R. A., Albaum, G., & Ridgway, N. (1989). Consumers who buy from direct sales companies. *Journal of Retailing, 65*(2), 273-286.

Raymond, M. A. (1990). *Generating repeat sales and increasing customer retention in direct selling companies.* Unpublished working paper, Direct Selling Education Foundation, Washington, DC.

Schultz, D. (1992). The direct/database marketing challenge to fixed-location retailers. In R. A. Peterson (Ed.), *The future of U.S. retailing: An agenda for the 21st century* (pp. 165-186). New York: Quorum Books.

Sharma, S., Bearden, W. O., & Teel, J. E. (1983). Differential effects of in-home shopping methods. *Journal of Retailing, 59,* 29-51.

Stone, B. (1988). *Successful direct marketing methods* (4th ed.). Lincolnwood, IL: NTC Books.

Talarzyk, W. W., & Widing, R. E., III. (1982a). *Introduction to and issues with videotex: Implications for marketing.* Working paper (WPS 82-16), Ohio State University, College of Administrative Sciences.

Talarzyk, W. W., & Widing, R. E., III. (1982b). *Viewdata project reviews.* Working paper (WPS 82-18), Ohio State University, College of Administrative Sciences.

Taylor, R. (1978). Marilyn's friends and Rita's customers: A study of party-selling as play and as work. *Sociological Review, 26*(3), 573-611.

Thistlethwaite, P. W., Norvell, D. G., Kornendowski, A., Billingsley, D., & Epperson, C. (1984). *Direct selling in midamerica.* Unpublished working paper, Direct Selling Education Foundation, Washington, DC.

Tootelian, D. H. (1975). Potential impact of "cooling-off" laws on direct-to-home selling. *Journal of Retailing, 51,* 61-70, 114.

Wolf, F. M. (1986). *Meta-analysis: Quantitative methods for research synthesis.* Beverly Hills, CA: Sage Publications Inc.

Wotruba, T. R. (1989). The effect of goal-setting on the performance of independent sales agents in direct selling. *Journal of Personal Selling and Sales Management, 9*(1), 22-29.

Wotruba, T. R. (1990a). Full-time vs. part-time salespeople: A comparison on job satisfaction, performance, and turnover in direct selling. *International Journal of Research in Marketing, 7,* 97-108.

Wotruba, T. R. (1990b). The relationship of job image, performance, and job satisfaction to inactivity-proneness of direct salespeople. *Journal of the Academy of Marketing Science, 18*(2), 113-121.

Wotruba, T. R. (1992). Direct selling in the year 2000. In R. A. Peterson (Ed.), *The future of U.S. retailing: An agenda for the 21st century* (pp. 187-216). New York: Quorum Books.

Wotruba, T. R., & Tyagi, P. K. (1991). Met expectations and turnover in direct selling. *Journal of Marketing, 55,* 24-35.

World Federation of Direct Selling Associations. (1990). *Worldwide direct sales data.* Washington, DC: Author.